REVOLUTION IN PERU:

MARIÁTEGUI

AND THE MYTH

by JOHN M. BAINES

Published for the
Latin American Studies Program
by
The University of Alabama Press
University, Alabama

CONTENTS

Introduction

It is not easy to write an introduction for a book which one has not read, especially a study dealing with José Carlos Mariátegui. But when the request comes from the author, my friend John M. Baines—whom I know through his admiration of Mariátegui—I am more than happy to do so. As a Peruvian, I am grateful to him for the study of this great national figure of ours which Mr. Baines has been pursuing for some years, and which he now makes public in this book.

Peru is a country with a great history. Before the Incas, numerous cultures existed which contributed to the Inca Empire. These cultures form the biological and cultural heritage which, to a greater or lesser degree, determine the characteristic attributes of today's Peruvians. According to recent discoveries, the pre-Incan cultural horizons were many—dating back 21,000 years. Genetic differences are quite varied. And if we add to this not only the contributions of the Hispanic Conquest and colonization, but also those of the Negroes and Chinese (which the colony and Republic imported as slave laborers) we have a cultural mosaic scattered throughout all the territory. The geographic environment also influences the inhabitants of present-day Peru due to the extremes of its harshness and mildness. Still, sufficient time has not passed for Peruvians to achieve a racial and cultural mixture which is more or less homogenous and consensual.

To become familiar with, and to study, all of these factors in Peru is not only to delve into the social sciences, which like geography present a formidable challenge, but to enter into and develop comparative studies of other societies as well. This singular purpose demands not only clear intelligence by whoever undertakes these studies, but a great desire as well. For one cannot master all the disciplines which are necessary for this knowledge.

José Carlos Mariátegui was a brilliant man possessed of lucid intelligence; his sickness, which accounted for his physical immobility, gave him longer hours for work and study. The understanding of Marxism—which he came to embrace without pretense—provided him with a dialectic view facilitating a clearing of the intellectual pathways which until then were quite obscure. One must admire the loftiness with which he treats M. V. Villarán, Javier Prado, and García Calderón when commenting upon their works. While their ideas were contrary to his own, in spite of this he wrote . . . "Again I repeat that I am not an impartial and objective critic. My opinions are nourished by my ideas, by my feelings, by my passions . . ."

To see Peru as Mariátegui saw it is extremely difficult. The decade of the 1920's did not offer all that we have today as a basis for knowledge. Ancient and profound Peru was intuitively sensed by Mariátegui rather than seen and studied by him. I am of the opinion that Mariátegui relied upon those powerful faculties of a keenness of mind and intuition. The understanding of his works, the perception of problems and his proposals for resolving those problems, are only now being sensed. His Marxist criteria and his style were as unique as his thought, his sentences, his aphorisms:

> "Our Revolution will not be an imitation or copy, but a heroic creation."
> "We shall Peruvianize Peru."

Thus, this is how we Peruvians of today understand Mariátegui. And I think that many of us, though we be as different as

Peru's geography, act and work following these aphorisms of Mariátegui either through understanding or conviction—or perhaps simply by intuition. Because we love Peru, we shall struggle for its Peruvianization.

Lima, Peru
April, 1971

Juan Mejía Baca

 Preface

This book is a study of one man and the impact that he and his ideas had on Peru. As such, I have attempted to write not only a political biography, but to relate that biography to the ideas of social change developed by José Carlos Mariátegui during his lifetime. This is not an easy task, especially when dealing with a self-proclaimed revolutionary whose thoughts are not always cogent or logically formulated. Revolutionaries are not usually logical men. Rather, they seek to mobilize their respective societies for change. Often, as in the case of Mariátegui, they give name and substance to "the nation." In this respect men such as Mariátegui are often the catalytic elements that introduce the ferment of change into traditional societies. This study attempts to probe the first stirrings of this ferment in Peru.

It should be noted that this book would have never been attempted without the encouragement of teachers and colleagues at the University of Wisconsin. Charles W. Anderson and Earl M. Aldrich provided the encouragement and criticism so necessary during crucial stages of research. Thanks are also due to Norman P. Sacks and John L. Phelan, whose initial guidance pointed me in the direction of this study. Finally, I would like to thank Juan Mejía Baca for the many courtesies he extended me while in Lima and during the final stages of this book. José Carlos Mariátegui, Jr., Director of the *Empresa Editora Amauta,* graciously gave permission to quote from his father's works.

Financial assistance was provided by the Ibero-American
Studies Committee through the Ford Foundation grant for
studies in international programs through the University of
Wisconsin. The Social Science Foundation of the University of
Denver provided funds for field research during the summer of
1969. While Professors Anderson and Aldrich have made an
especially deep impression on what is written here, I alone bear
the responsibility for any errors.

University of Wyoming   JOHN M. BAINES
January, 1972

1

The Revolutionary Idea
in Peru

A major theme in the political discourse of Latin America is that of "revolution." Yet no precise definition of this theme exists, even though it appears in the political rhetoric of most of the Latin American countries. One must determine what meaning this idea conveys in each specific political context. In general, revolution implies class warfare, violence, and the elimination of certain political groups from positions of power and authority. But in some Latin American contexts, revolution may mean a military coup that merely signals a change of personnel within the ruling elite.[1] The list of possible "revolutionary" situations in Latin America is practically endless. Therefore, if one wishes to assess the meaning and significance of revolution as an idea and an integral part of the political process, it is necessary to specify *which* political system is the focus of inquiry.

One of the confusing aspects of Peruvian politics is the fact that practically every contender for power is a self-proclaimed revolutionary. However, Peruvian revolutionary groups do not follow the same patterns of behavior. Some, like the National Liberation Front (FLN) are avowedly Maoist and call for the violent destruction of the state in seizing power. Others, such as the Popular American Revolutionary Alliance (APRA) have become reform-oriented nationalists seeking power through the electoral process. Even the military regime, which took over in October 1968, proclaims itself revolutionary. This commitment to revolution by groups throughout the political spectrum could

lead one to think that being revolutionary has no real significance—that this is mere political rhetoric. This is not the
case, especially in Peru. The significance of being a revolutionary cannot be lightly dismissed as meaningless, as we shall see.
Let us examine this commitment to revolution more closely in
order to determine what its significance is, and has been in
Peruvian politics.

This book is an assessment of the meaning of revolution in
the Peruvian political context. It traces the development of this
concept through the first three decades of the twentieth century.
It was during this period that the idea of revolution became a
dominant theme in Peruvian politics. In this volume we shall
be concerned with the life and writings of Peru's most noted
revolutionary theorist, José Carlos Mariátegui (1895–1930).

Mariátegui has long been recognized as a major figure in the
development of modern Latin American political thought. He
has been eulogized by the communists as the precursor of a
communist revolution in the Southern Hemisphere, though
other Marxist writers antedated Mariátegui, namely Juan B.
Justo and Luis Emilio Recabarren.[2] However, until quite
recently Mariátegui has been neglected by North American
scholars. Little is known of his life, and only one of his major
works has appeared in English translation.* This has been
unfortunate for one can only understand the Peruvian political
process by being fully aware of the significance of Mariátegui
in the making of the Peruvian ideology of revolution.

The development of the modern concept of revolution did not
burst forth in Peru solely from the ideas of Mariátegui. Rather,
this developmental process began during the closing decades of
the nineteenth century in the writings of Manuel González
Prada.[3] González Prada's view of revolution was quite differ-

*Seven Interpretive Essays on Peruvian Reality, translated by Marjory
Urquidi, Introduction by Jorge Basadre (Austin: University of Texas Press,
1971).

ent from that which motivated the leaders of the early nineteenth century independence movements. Basically, the early nineteenth century concept of revolution signified a *political*, not a social revolution. The independence leaders were concerned principally with replacing the elites in positions of power and authority. They wanted to substitute creole rule for rule by the foreign-born Spanish authorities. Moreover, they did not seek to alter the social and economic structures of their respective societies.

By the late nineteenth century, intellectuals like González Prada became concerned with political *and* social revolution. González Prada desired nothing less than a complete restructuring of Peruvian society. It was the commitment to thoroughgoing social and political change, first articulated by González Prada, that became the theoretical point of departure for his successor, José Carlos Mariátegui.

The vague exhortations of González Prada were taken by Mariátegui and developed into specific proposals and justifications for a total change of Peruvian society. In doing so, Mariátegui set the tone and direction for radical reform political ideologies that have continued down to the present. Yet he was not a political theorist in the Western European tradition. He had no university education; nor did he possess a highly disciplined intellect. Mariátegui was primarily a journalist, essayist, and in the later years of his life a political activist. He did not develop a comprehensive theory regarding the nature and purpose of politics in Peru. Indeed, Mariátegui's revolutionary ideas were evidence of his deep distrust of politics—a trait that is not unique among revolutionaries. If this is so, why then has Mariátegui been so important a force? The answer lies not in the logic or coherence of his ideas, but in the fact that Mariátegui was one of the first to clearly grasp the the fundamental problems facing his society. Moreover, he was the first Peruvian to propose specifically nationalist *and* Marxist solutions to those problems.

There were two central questions that concerned Mariátegui—racial and cultural pluralism, and the related problem
of organizing society so that economic growth would occur.[4]
None of these problems could be solved unless a legitimate
political order were established. This, in Mariátegui's view,
had been a continuing problem since the Conquest. The Indian, comprising some two thirds of the total population of Peru,
had remained outside the political life of the country and had
only been a marginal participant in the economy. *Mestizos,* the
racial product of the European and the Indian, had few opportunities for advancement. Positions of prestige and authority
were held by a small number of white descendants of the Spanish conquerors, or later European immigrants.

Mariátegui wanted to change completely those conditions.
He attempted to chart a new course for Peru through the creation of a new social and political order based upon the Indian and the mestizo, *not* the alien white European. He wanted to
provide that sense of unity and purpose which would create the
basis for political legitimacy—a condition which he believed
had been absent from Peru since the destruction of the Inca
Empire in the sixteenth century. In order to accomplish this
task, Mariátegui sought to develop an ideology that would
unify the powerless elements of Peruvian society: the Indian,
the mestizo, and the disenchanted intellectuals. His ideology,
then, was designed to bridge this racial and cultural gap in
order to create a new political force that would be truly
national and therefore legitimate.

The themes developed by Mariátegui in the decade of the
1920's have become the symbols of the basic commitment to
social change (*revolución*) in Peru. These form the basis of the
ideology of Victor Raúl Haya de la Torre, the founder of
APRA. And they have also formed the core of the ideological
structure of the Popular Action party (Acción Popular) of the
recently ousted President Fernando Belaúnde Terry. Homage
to Mariátegui is paid by practically every political group. None

can hope to gain power by popular mandate without at least voicing symbolic adherence to the goals of land-reform, integration of the Indian into the social fabric of the nation, and the development of the economy under *Peruvian* auspices—all goals first articulated clearly by Mariátegui.[5]

There are two points that should be made regarding Mariátegui's role as a political theorist and activist. In my view, he represents the type of personality described by Daniel J. Lerner in, *The Passing of Traditional Society.*[6] Mariátegui was a transition figure in the process of social change; the man between the worlds of tradition and modernity. As such, he retained many of the values and mores of the very society that he was determined to change. As a mestizo, he was caught between Peru's two mutually antagonistic worlds—the Indian and the white European. He was a product of these two cultures, yet not wholly a part of either. His life and writings represent an attempt to resolve this antagonism by changing his society into one that was compatible with his own world view.

As we know, Lerner was concerned with the process of social change in the Middle East. In gathering his data and developing a typology of social change he relied mainly on interviews and attitude surveys. Lerner attempted to treat the phenomenon of social change as one of "mass" political behavior. In this typology, he described a type of transitional figure which he termed "The Spokesman." Lerner viewed this personality as the key agent in the transition process for entire communities.

"The Spokesman" [Lerner wrote] is he who defines new identities for changing persons, reshapes old expectancies and formulates new demands to fit their lifeways. . . . It is the Spokesman who unlocks the chambers of the mind, releases the wellsprings of desire, opens new relationships between self and society. He discovers for men-on-the-move, in Nasser's phrase, "who we are and what our role is to be."[7]

Mariátegui was precisely this type of figure identified by Lerner. However, Mariátegui did not personally lead his movement in a successful seizure of power. His early death prevented this. But he did inspire others to seek the goals which he outlined. In word and deed, he spoke for an entire generation of Peruvian men-on-the-move.

Mariátegui's attempts to resolve the problems of racial and cultural pluralism, and his concern for economic development, must be viewed with an eye to Peru's cultural heritage. His thought bears the imprint of a culture that for centuries was steeped in authoritarian Spanish political traditions and religious mysticism. He himself reflected that heritage when he asserted that the primary purpose of society was the spiritual regeneration of man.[8] His ideal society would transform the moral *and* material life of man. Spiritual and temporal ends became fused in Mariátegui's Marxist doctrine of national revolution.

The revolutionary themes which Mariátegui developed were uniquely Peruvian; but they were not wholly unlike those of other revolutionary "Spokesmen" in today's developing world. He attempted to find solutions to the universal political questions of national integration and the establishment of a legitimate political order; this legitimacy was to be based on the historical, racial, and cultural heritage of his country. He tried to develop a truly *national* ideology of social change through an eclectic recombination of Marxist, Hispanic, and indigenous Peruvian themes. His efforts to build an ideology that would bridge the gap of racial and cultural pluralism are not unique. Nor was his emphasis on the communal nature of man as the foundation for a legitimate polity. Such ideology-building is not unlike that of Senegal's Leopold Senghor, the concept of Indian Socialism developed by Nehru, or the creation of the "new man" by the Cuban Revolution of Fidel Castro.

This ideology of Peruvian revolution developed by Mariátegui consists of four basic elements.

1. A commitment to obtain a better material and moral way of life for the mass of the people through fundamental change of the social system.

2. A willingness to adopt non-Hispanic, non-Peruvian ideas to explain existing social, economic, and political conditions; and to use these explanations also to justify changing those conditions.

3. An attempt to create a new sense of national identity through the synthesis of these ideas.

4. A commitment to obtain the material benefits of a modern, secular, individualistic, industrialized society, while retaining the commitment to corporatism, and the moral and spiritual purpose of that society.[9]

These elements form the core of Peruvian revolutionary thought, and they still survive today. Indeed they are quite evident in the revolutionary goals outlined by the present military regime of General Juan Velasco Alvarado.[10] Yet Peru still has not experienced that revolution which Mariátegui envisioned. The following chapters provide some insights into the reasons for the survival of Mariátegui's ideas. In addition to tracing the development of the revolutionary idea in Peru, we shall explore some of the possible answers to the question of why Peru has not had the revolution that seemed so inevitable to Mariátegui. We begin with the "traditional" Peru of the turn of the century.

2

Antecedents of Revolution

The wars of independence, which led to the definitive break with imperial Spain, left the army and the Church as the only surviving institutions in Peru that were capable of directing the destiny of the new republic. The army in particular emerged as a powerful institution. For almost five decades after independence was won, Peru was governed by a succession of military strong-men whose power was buttressed by the support of the Church. Indeed, this basic post-independence pattern of rule has survived down to the present day. The army and the Church have traditionally remained the most powerful forces in Peruvian politics.[1]

The most enlightened of the military *caudillos* that ruled Peru in the decades following independence was undoubtedly Ramón Castilla who served two terms as president (1845–1851 and 1855–1862). Castilla was part Indian and the success of his first administration provided some small outlet for upward mobility for the mestizo elements in Peru.

During both his administrations Castilla was obsessed with the idea of a strong military force to preserve and protect internal order and Peruvian sovereignty in the hemisphere. But more important were the economic and social changes wrought by Castilla on Peruvian life. For the first time since independence, a modicum of economic order was introduced into the budget and government services. Castilla prepared and sent to the assembly the first national budget in Peruvian history. In addition, a general accounting bureau was established to over-

see expenditures. National statistics were gathered for the first
time, and the bureaucracy could depend on regular salaries.

Economically, Castilla fared less well. During his first
administration the great guano deposits were exploited for fer-
tilizers, and the nitrate deposits of southern Peru began to be
developed. British and French developers advanced the Peruvian government loans for shipments to be sent to Europe. This
income was indeed a windfall for a Peru that was hard-pressed
by foreign debts. However, the advances were used to pay these
foreign debts and cover internal expenditures. Little of this new
income went into internal economic development. The economy
became *less* rather than more self-sustaining.

Castilla did little to foster internal economic development for
he and his advisers were convinced that a policy of laissez faire
was best for Peru. Thus, as the guano boom brought Peru
more revenue than ever before, the nation became poorer. The
foreign debt rose, and the earnings from the guano beds were
mortgaged further and further into the future. This, coupled
with the Castilla regime's frequent border wars, almost completely bankrupted the economy.

Socially, the Castilla regime deeply affected Peruvian life as
well. During his second term of office he freed the some twenty
thousand Negro slaves and compensated the owners up to forty
percent of the value of the freedmen. Yet Castilla later bowed
to the pressures of the landowners and agreed to import Chinese immigrants under a bondage system. By 1875 some eighty
thousand Chinese laborers had been brought into Peru.[2] Indian
tribute taxes were suppressed by Castilla, thus depriving the
national government of about ten percent of its revenue. Local
governments were made even more dependent on the central
government than previously since only a portion of the tribute
collected by local authorities went to the central government
prior to suppression of the tribute. Yet one cannot judge Castilla too harshly. For while other Andean countries were tear-
ing themselves apart in liberal-conservative struggles, Castilla

managed to steer a middle course that kept the two opposing
forces from engaging in civil war. Indeed this ability of Castilla
to compromise and establish contacts with both factions enabled him to leave the presidency after his second term having
saved Peru from civil war. Yet he had inadvertently laid the
groundwork for economic disaster that would haunt Peru well
into the twentieth century.

Prior to 1872, civilian participation in politics through political parties was practically non-existent. Governments changed
hands through a process of civil wars waged between rival military factions. However, new potential bases of political participation were being laid in the 1840's and 1850's, when the
great guano and nitrate booms occurred. A new class of businessmen and entrepreneurs began to emerge. The power of the
old land-holding aristrocracy began to be challenged by these
new entrepreneurs whose fortunes did not lie in landed estates.
Their economic success depended on the growth of commerce
and industry, especially guano and nitrate; and they saw their
futures threatened by capricious military rule, endless civil
wars, and systematic looting of the public treasury. They
formed a new political organization opposed to the inept rule of
military regimes. The new party, the Partido Civilista, gained
sufficient strength to have its candidate elected president in
1872. However, the electoral campaign erupted into a bloody
civil war between army factions and the navy which supported
the civilistas. The new party retained control of the government
until the disastrous defeats of the Second War of the Pacific
brought on a resurgence of army rule.

The Second War of the Pacific is the great watershed in
modern Peruvian history and the conflict is bitterly remembered to this day. Initially, hostilities broke out over a bound-
ary dispute between Chile and Bolivia, and between Peru and
Chile over control of the desert nitrate areas. The details of the
conflict are not necessary for our purposes; it is sufficient to
note that the war, lasting from 1879 to 1884, was a nightmare

for Peru. The army suffered defeat after defeat, culminating in the most devastating event in Peruvian national history—the Chilean occupation of Lima from 1881 to 1884. Hostilities finally ended in 1884, leaving Peru destitute, deprived of her nitrate holdings, and once again torn by civil war. Though an armistice was agreed to, the final settlement did not come about until 1929, when an international commission of arbitration imposed a settlement that was bitterly opposed by most Peruvians.[3]

The war heralded a period of military rule by a now thoroughly discredited army, and almost immediately a new coalition of conservatives and anti-militarists was formed in opposition. This alliance was to prove a durable one, lasting through the second decade of the twentieth century. The old civilistas were absorbed into this new party—the Democratic Party. Actually the base of these two parties was similar, being composed of landowners, wealthy miners, and businessmen. Under the leadership of Nicolás de Piérola, the party staged a coup in 1895 and ousted the military rulers. Under Piérola, Peru made significant economic gains and was efficiently administered. A period of constitutional government began which was to endure until the Leguía coup of 1919. Yet if the political process was characterized by constitutionalism, the pattern of rule remained the same. Civilian strong-men merely replaced military ones. Oligarchic rule, which now included rich businessmen, continued. The liberal fiction of popular elections endured, though the electoral base was indeed narrow. The government was still composed of men who looked after the interests of the propertied and the wealthy.

The year 1919 marked the end of this comparatively peaceful era of constitutional government in Peru. It also marked the beginning of revolutionary agitation that kept the republic in turmoil for the next decade. Augusto B. Leguía toppled the civilista-Democratic Party coalition, and installed himself as president. Paradoxically, Leguía staged a coup *after* he had

been constitutionally elected president. Leguía was an econo-
mist, not an army man; but his roots were in the new class of
entrepreneurs, not the landed aristocracy. He had served as
minister of finance in the early 1900's and as president from
1908 to 1912. The sources of his support remained among the
newly emergent business interests and wealthy British investors. (Prior to the 1920's, Britain dominated the Peruvian
economy.)

Leguía offered these business groups the prospect of a stable
regime that would encourage economic growth and foreign
investment. This position also gained him at least the tolerance
of the army in his bid for power. Once Leguía seized power,
political opponents were rooted out and packed off into exile.
Labor unrest was brutally curbed by the police. Thus began
one of the most economically progressive, and politically re-
pressive, dictatorships in Peru's history—the *oncenio*.

The shock of the Second War of the Pacific created extensive
intellectual as well as political ferment. Peru's humiliating
defeat at the hands of Chile caused many hitherto non-political
intellectuals to think about the causes of such national calam-
ity. This soul-searching intellectual movement of self-criticism
was led by Manuel González Prada, an aristocratic intellectual who had renounced his upper-class heritage. This movement of self-criticism became a forerunner of the Peruvian
political movements for social change in the early twentieth
century. Many of the leaders of these later movements were
followers of González Prada, and all were influenced by the
wave of intellectual ferment which he helped to launch. It was
he who first, and most clearly, pointed out the bankruptcy of
Peru's political institutions—the personalistic, faction-ridden
party system, a ruling elite that sought only personal aggran-
dizement, and a system of government that permitted men in
the cities to go hungry, while the Indian, two thirds of the total
population, remained in a state of feudal serfdom.

González Prada was the leading figure of a new "literature

of disillusionment," which grew after 1884 and attacked the ills so apparent in Peruvian society. He applied his keen intelligence and acid pen to the task of arresting and reversing this trend of moral and spiritual decay which he thought permeated Peruvian life. As his writings became more popular, a coterie of disciples began to surround him, attracted by his personal magnetism and thunderous calls for sweeping social change.[4] The political nature of González Prada's writings was unmistakable. He was not concerned with the artistic aspects of the writer's craft, as were his Modernist and Romantic contemporaries in Latin America. Nor was he intent on disguising the political themes that he had developed. He painted them boldly for all to read, and developed the essay as a primary form of political expression. Four major themes dominated his thought, and these became the intellectual point of departure for Mariátegui. These were:

1. National integration based on the indigenous Inca heritage.

2. Land reform and elimination of the *hacienda* system.

3. Criticism of Peru's ruling elite for their European cultural bias.

4. Criticism of the Catholic Church for its involvement in politics.

González Prada voiced deep concern for the condition of the Indian masses. He glorified the Inca heritage, and particularly their social and political organization. This concern for the Indian led him to attack the land tenure system which not only held the Indian in bondage, but kept the emerging middle class from acquiring land as well. González Prada also criticized the ruling elite for their failure to place any value in Peru's unique cultural heritage. Finally and most vehemently, he attacked the Church as a political and social institution. According to Gon-

zález Prada, this potentially powerful force for good had violated its own tenets. Moreover, its teachings bore little rele-
vance to the problems faced in the daily life of the individual. It
had become a corrupting force in Peruvian society. It had lost
sight of the moral and spiritual ends of man.[5]

González Prada broke a traditional pattern in Latin American thought that rejected the idea of a scientific theory of history. This idea, so prominent in nineteenth-century European
thought, was a bit too deterministic to be accepted in an intellectual milieu steeped in Thomistic and Romantic tradition. In
this respect, González Prada was indeed a precursor of Mariátegui, and it is doubtful that Mariátegui's ideas would have
gained such popularity had not González Prada laid the intellectual groundwork.

González Prada had travelled extensively in Europe and had
absorbed some of the Marxist and Syndicalist ideas which were
then so popular on the Continent. He know little about economics, but had become obsessed with the idea of revolution as
the panacea for all social ills. He believed that a spontaneous
revolution would destroy the old social structure and somehow
make his nation whole again once it had been violently torn
apart. To accomplish this great task, he envisioned an alliance
of workers, Indians, and intellectuals. The intellectuals were to
be the guiding force for "they serve as a light." But even as
revolutions were "implanted from above", they should "come
from below."[6] Clearly, the intellectuals' task was one of mobilization and directing the revolution—a task in which Mariátegui also believed.

The role of the Indian in this revolutionary alliance was to
prove the most difficult to explain. Here it must be noted that
González Prada, and most Peruvian intellectuals, had little
first-hand knowledge of the Indian. The idealization of the
Indian which has become a hallmark of Peruvian political
thought has been essentially based on second-hand knowledge
of the Indian and his culture. Most intellectuals had their roots

in the Spanish side of Peruvian culture. They could not speak Quechua, the language of the Inca which still survives to this day in the highland communities. Moreover, until fairly recently their only sources on Indian culture and society were the colonial accounts written during and immediately after the Spanish conquest. Many of these accounts, written by missionaries, were intended to convince the Spanish crown that the Indians should not be enslaved nor their culture destroyed. The idealization of the Indian begun in the middle of the sixteenth century was renewed with greater vigor in the late nineteenth century. Yet it was an almost impossible task to bring the Indian into a social revolutionary movement, when the leaders of the movement knew little of the indigenous people and could not communicate with them in their own language.

González Prada sought to accomplish the impossible task by developing the concept of a two-stage revolution. The revolution was to begin in the cities among the workers and intellectuals, and then spread to the countryside as the apathetic Indian masses were aroused.[7] González Prada vigorously rejected the idea of racial inferiority that was commonly held in late nineteenth-century Europe. His idealization of the Inca can be seen as a partial rejoinder to the racist arguments of such men as Gobineau. González Prada also rejected the idea that education was the key to bettering the Indian's lot. Revolution was, in his view, the *only* way that the Indian could better his condition. The landed aristocracy would never permit the Indian to advance from his state of servitude. A peaceful social revolution was, therefore, out of the question. "The problem of the Indian," he stated, "is economic and social more than educational. . . . The Indian will be redeemed by his own efforts, not by the humanizing of his oppressors."[8]

For all his idealism and the messianic call for spontaneous revolution, González Prada was not completely blind to reality. He saw that the long centuries of isolation and servitude had sapped the Indian's moral strength and initiative. This was where the intellectuals would play a key role. They were to awaken the Indian's desire for self-achievement. The Indian's total outlook on life had to be changed. He had to be made to believe that he could effect a change of his life.[9] Apparently the example of successful revolution in the cities was to bridge the gap of understanding and communication that existed between the Indian and the rest of Peruvian society. Despite humanistic arguments, the Indian for González Prada remained a symbol, an abstraction.

The young men that were attracted to González Prada became known as part of "the generation of 1919." They, too, saw the Indian in the same symbolic light. They accepted the arguments of their master on faith rather than logic. They were possessed with a messianic belief in the inevitability of the revolution that would change Peru. But unlike their mentor, they became participants in the political process by founding political organizations that attempted to bring about this revolution.[10] José Carlos Mariátegui was a youth who flitted on the fringe of this group of young intellectuals that believed that they held the destiny of a new Peru in their hands. González Prada died in 1918, and it was not until some ten years later that Mariátegui cogently summed up his influence.

> González Prada was more a literary figure than a political one. But the political transcendence of his work may be greater than the literary. . . . His individualist spirit . . . was not adequate for the direction of a vast collective work [i.e. the development of a revolutionary political program]. He was an accusor, not a builder . . . but . . . in the depths of this Parnassian there is a romantic who never despairs of the power of the spirit.[11]

It was this "power of the spirit" that González Prada had injected into the young men that followed him, along with vague political ideas of revolution. It was Mariátegui and this "generation of 1919" which moved from a rather naïve intellectual involvement to a course of a more militant political activism.

3

The Generation
of 1919 Emerges

On July 14, 1895, the year of Nicolás de Piérola's successful
military coup, José Carlos Mariátegui was born in Lima.[1] The
boy's father, Francisco Mariátegui, was a minor civil servant
who could give his son little more than a well-known Basque
name. The Mariátegui family has many branches in Peru, each
claiming that their roots go back to Francisco Javier Mariátegui, the Liberal president of the first constituent assembly of
the republic, and a writer of modest talents. Mariátegui's
father was a shadowy figure to his son. He left the family
shortly after José Carlos' birth and moved to northern Peru,
leaving the family destitute. He was never seen again, and the
family became dependent on the meagre resources of Mariátegui's mother, María Amalia La Chira.[2] Mariátegui never
came to know his father, and throughout his life his mother
exerted a strong influence on her son.

José Carlos was a sickly child, and his health remained delicate throughout his short life span of thirty-five years. Shortly
after his birth, the family moved to the coastal town of Huacho
some thirty miles north of Lima. There he began his elemen-
tary school education. While at school he suffered a knee injury
which sent him on the first of innumerable trips to the hospital.
The injury could not be treated adequately in Huacho, so in
1902 the family returned to Lima where several operations
were performed.

After several months of convalescence, Mariátegui could
resume walking, but with a limp that was permanent. The

knee injury was the beginning of a life of constant physical suffering. The boy was afflicted with what would later be diagnosed as tuberculosis of the bone, a disease that robbed him of physical energy and caused him to become an invalid at the age of thirty. Throughout his life Mariátegui was faced with the prospect of an early death. Yet he always avoided discussing the subject, and never permitted anyone to speak of it in his presence.[3] From early childhood he was deeply thoughtful, even morose. His constant physical pain and the financial troubles of his family did little to distract him from such preoccupations.

José Carlos grew to manhood almost without having gone through a period of adolescence. He left school at the age of fourteen. A secondary education at that time was a luxury that only few could afford. The family needed every bit of money just to survive. (Mariátegui had a brother Julio César, and a sister Guillermina.) In 1909, at the age of fourteen, he went to work as a copy boy at the newspaper, La Prensa. Now the family's fortunes rose a bit, for Mariátegui's salary augmented the income that his mother's sewing brought in. This first job was a decisive step in his life. It set the pattern for his career as a journalist and essayist; moreover, his formal education was ended. In a society where an education was the traditional path to status, material success, and social mobility, Mariátegui found himself at a serious disadvantage. He was determined to overcome this handicap posed by his lack of the "proper" credentials in the newspaper and literary world. But his lack of formal education plagued him, and in later years he often referred to himself defiantly as an autodidáctico—a self-taught man.[4]

La Prensa was then one of the most prestigious newspapers in Lima, and also one of the most outspoken opponents of the civilista-Democratic coalition rule. Don Alberto Ullóa Cisneros, the owner and editor, took notice of the thin boy with the dark, piercing eyes and promoted him to a better position. In

1910 Mariátegui became a proofreader and assistant to the linotype operator. The newspaper was the beginning of many lifelong friendships for Mariátegui. It was here that he got his first taste of Lima's intellectual climate. The promising young writers Abraham Valdelomar, Félix del Valle, and César Falcón also wrote for the paper, and the four soon became fast friends. They often whiled away the evening hours in long discussions at the Palaise Concert, a favorite meeting place for the literary lights of Lima.

As a proofreader Mariátegui had some opportunities to write short articles to fill in gaps in the paper's news columns. These first unsigned articles usually concerned sporting events and police news. In 1914 he began to publish his first essays and poems using the popular literary device of the time, the pseudonym. For the next decade Mariátegui's work appeared under several pseudonyms.[5] Yet Mariátegui, a mestizo of the lower middle class, could never break into the circle of the intellectual aristocracy. This was one of the reasons why he was only on the fringe of the intellectual group that surrounded González Prada. In Mariátegui's day an intellectual was one who was pursuing, or who had a university education. By definition this meant that he was a member of the upper class. Nevertheless, some young intellectuals accepted him in their circle, and through them (Falcón, Valdelomar, and del Valle) he became acquainted with the intellectual currents in Peru.

In 1916 Mariátegui and his young friends founded a journal called *Colónida*. They sought to create a new intellectual climate in Peru quite apart from the academism, the class consciousness, and the other-wordly attitude which they thought was the hallmark of the decadence of Peruvian art and letters. This was not a new technique on their part. Literary journals were founded and dissolved almost every day in Peru. *Colónida* followed the same pattern. It collapsed after just four issues. The journal created no new wave of intellectual excitement. Its contributors used the same obscure, byzantine style to criticize

the obscure, byzantine style and content of the then leading
Latin American literary trend—Modernism.[6]

The leading figures in the short-lived *Colónida* movement
were Mariátegui, Julio de la Paz, and Abraham Valdelomar.
Valdelomar was the oldest, the most widely travelled, and more
politically oriented than the others. He had been attracted to
politics while a student, and in 1913 had led a student-worker
demonstration through Lima. In 1914 he went to Europe and
returned a follower of D'Annunzio. The spirit of the Italian
D'Annunzian belief that politics could be influenced by the
intellectual's pen was quite consistent with González Prada's
arguments. Through Valdelomar these two sets of ideas became
fused in the literary movement that was *Colónida*. Mariátegui
and Valdelomar were great friends until the latter's death in
1919. Undoubtedly, it was through his close association with
Valdelomar that Mariátegui first began to think in political
terms.[7]

The transition from political detachment to involvement and
activism was perhaps more difficult for Mariátegui than his
colleagues. He felt a deep attachment to his mother, and
through her a deep attachment to Roman Catholicism. His
companions had rejected any organized religion—they felt that
the task of building a new Peru founded on vague principles of
universal social justice had more transcendent value than anything offered by religion, especially Catholicism.

It took Mariátegui some time to come around to this position. For two years he wrestled with the dilemma posed by
attachment to his new friends and their cause, his loyalty to his
mother and through her, his ties with Catholicism. His writings in *Colónida* reflect this internal struggle. They dwell on
the mysteries of faith, and the search for a direct knowledge of
God. Mariátegui was greatly influenced by the experiences and
example of the sixteenth century Spanish mystics, Saint Teresa
of Ávila, and Saint John of the Cross, founders of the Order of
Descalced Carmelites. In 1916, hoping to resolve this internal

conflict, Mariátegui entered the Monastery of the Descalced Carmelites in Lima for a solemn retreat. Yet the solitude of the monastic cell could provide no answers. He was searching for a relationship with God that would explain his life and give it a sense of meaning and direction.[8] The search proved fruitless; and he looked elsewhere for his life's meaning and purpose.

Following the collapse of *Colónida,* Mariátegui was forced to seek new employment. He became co-director of the new sporting magazine *El Turf.* His articles, which began to appear in the new publication in 1916, gave little indication of the internal struggle that he was trying to resolve.[9] Along with the *El Turf* assignment he also began writing for the newspaper *El Tiempo.* These unsigned articles appeared in a section on current events in Peru entitled "Voices." Here one can trace his increasing involvement in political and social questions, and the religious conflict which still plagued him.[10]

The spirit of revolt against intellectual and social decadence did not die with *Colónida.* As soon as Mariátegui and his friends saved some money they continued their efforts in a new journal *Nuestra Época,* which they founded in 1918. The same *Colónida* group was still intact, but the content of their articles was now much more political than literary. Coinciding with the founding of *Nuestra Época,* Mariátegui ended his long association with *La Prensa.* He rejected the conservative ideas of its editor, and renounced his most commonly used pseudonym, Juan Croniquer—"under which he is known, and he has begged the pardon of God and the public for the many sins which he has committed under that name."[11] The year 1918 marks Mariátegui's definitive break with his "traditional" past as represented by his mother and the Roman Catholic religion. Yet the deep personal questions which had plagued him still continued to do so; they became for him social questions. He traced the tragedy of his own life and that of his family, to the evils of an archaic, unjust social system.[12]

Nuestra Época was even more ephemeral than *Colónida.* It

ran for only two issues, then folded for lack of funds. Mariátegui by this time had become disenchanted with the mildly
reformist editorial policy of *El Tiempo* and left the newspaper
in 1919. He and Falcón founded still another journal, *La
Razón* in the same year. *La Razón* was further to the left than
Nuestra Época, and called for the creation of a socialist society
as the answer to all of Peru's ills. Yet, paradoxically, *La Razón*
was published on the chancery press of the archbishop of Lima.
Vaguely Marxist in tone, *La Razón* called for the preparation
of a revolution. It rejected any idea of reforming the old social
system. Yet Mariátegui and his associates still had gone little
further than González Prada in developing an ideology and
program for action. They were still groping for a uniquely
Peruvian solution for Peru's social problems. By 1919 they had
found no such solution other than calling for the creation of a
"new" society vaguely termed "socialist."

   The idea of socialism was most likely Valdelomar's, since
probably none of the other members of the group even knew
what the term signified. Valdelomar had lived and studied in
Italy at the time when the anarchosyndicalist ideas of Sorel had
such a great impact. He had also been a student and admirer of
Benedetto Croce. It was probably Valdelomar who advanced
the propositions of non-cooperation with the existing "bourgeois-liberal" order, the necessity for a "myth" to guide and
strengthen the masses on the path to revolution, and the role of
the "audacious minority" of intellectuals that would lead the
revolution. These propositions went beyond those of González
Prada and seemed to provide a program for the implementation
of the ideas that the master had first developed. This new, militant approach had great appeal among the young men of *La
Razón.* They became fully converted to the goal of achieving
socialism (whatever that ill-defined term meant) as the revolutionary goal. For Mariátegui, the association with *La Razón*
and Valdelomar paved the way for his exposure to, and acceptance of, the radically new doctrine of revolutionary Marxism.

The carnage of World War I seemed to prove to Mariátegui and his friends that the old bourgeois-capitalist order was morally and politically bankrupt. Socialists in France and Germany had rejected the teachings of Marx by cooperating with their respective governments in the conduct of the war—thus proving that Marx's universal revolutionary class, the proletariat, still clung to its national loyalties. Mariátegui fully accepted the concept of a universal class, and leaned toward complete rejection of any cooperation with a feudal or bourgeois-liberal order. He believed that only the intellectuals could prepare the masses to assume their revolutionary role. His thoughts on socialism and its attainment through revolution changed in the 1920's. But Mariátegui never abandoned the idea of the primary role of an intellectual elite in guiding the movement.

The years 1918 and 1919 were times of great activity for Mariátegui and his associates. The discontent of the Peruvian workers grew as prosperity increased. Great profits were made by businessmen, mine owners, and plantation operators. But the workers did not share in these profits. During World War I the industrial powers needed the ores, cotton, rice, and sugar which countries like Peru could produce. The prices of these primary products soared on the world market during the war years. The Peruvian mines worked at full capacity, and the lands of the coast that produced food for domestic consumption were shifted to the cultivation of the more profitable export crops such as sugar and rice. Domestic food shortages resulted and ever increasing quantities of foodstuffs had to be imported. The cost of living rose dramatically in Peru while wages of miners, industrial, and agricultural workers remained at their pre-war level.[13] While wages were fixed, they had the purchasing power of about one-half of their 1914 level. By 1919 the situation exploded in a series of strikes and violence in the mines and major cities.

Mariátegui's group did not know what to do with the situation that presented itself. They knew that they must take advantage of the unrest to advance their cause. Yet they were undecided as to what that cause was, or how to attain it. Throughout the turbulent period of the 1919 strikes the group was in disarray, torn by internal disputes over strategy and leadership. While Mariátegui and his friends lent their editorial support to the striking workers, they could do little else. The situation taught them the value of effective organization and leadership—two qualities which they sadly lacked. They immediately set about to remedy that situation.

Throughout 1918 Mariátegui and César Falcón had tried to form a political organization but were unsuccessful. There were two basic splinter groups of intellectuals that had arisen from the literary-political movement which came to be known as "the generation of 1919." First there were those of Mariátegui's group who leaned toward socialism and political activism. Then there were those who had not been politicized, but still adhered to the pristine intellectual detachment of the nineteenth century. Paradoxically, they called themselves the Futurists. The Futurists were more a literary than a political movement. They held to the vague nihilism that characterized nineteenth century "literature of disillusionment" figures such as González Prada. The Futurists and Mariátegui's *La Razón* group lived in a loose alliance until 1918; each faction remained imbued with the idealistic notion of the fraternal unity of all intellectuals regardless of political opinion.[14] This bond of "fraternal unity" was suddenly broken in 1918.

The Futurists refused to join Mariátegui and Falcón in the formation of a para-political party. Finally, Mariátegui and his followers broke with them, accusing them of being politically sterile and lacking in ideological orientation. The Futurists also gave tacit support to the candidacy of Augusto Leguía, while Mariátegui and his followers opposed Leguía. Mariátegui also had initially supported Leguia's presidential candidacy, though he was not wildly enthusiastic about him. He considered him a lesser evil than the incumbent coalition government which he likened to the Spanish Carlists. In 1917 and 1918 Mariátegui probably saw Leguía as an expedient ally who could break the *civilista* hold on Peru. For some still unexplained reason, he moved to a position of complete opposition to Leguía in mid-1918.[15]

The greatest gap between Mariátegui and the Futurists was over the issue of timing and preparation for the revolution which each faction believed to be inevitable. The gap could not be bridged. The Futurists remained in the nineteenth century, while Mariátegui, as he later acknowledged, went a step further on the road to developing a theory of Peruvian socialism.[16] The *La Razón* faction ceased contributing articles to the Futurist journal *Germinal,* and in 1919 they formed the Committee of Socialist Propaganda headed by Mariátegui and Falcón. Some of the committee wanted to immediately form a Peruvian Socialist Party, but Mariátegui opposed the move. He apparently wanted to keep his options open. While he was fully committed to the creation of a political organization, he had not decided what *kind* of organization it should be. He thought that the basis of the organization should be its ideology, yet was uncertain as to just what that ideology should be. The Committee he thought, was a movement in search of such an ideology.

Augusto Leguía hastened the advent of his presidential term by staging a coup d'etat on July 14, 1919. Upon seizing power he immediately freed the imprisoned leaders of the labor movement. Though the workers had not actually won any substantive gains, they nevertheless staged a great victory march through the streets of Lima. They even stopped outside the office of *La Razón* and acclaimed Mariátegui for the support his journal had given them. Such support also earned the animosity of the archbishop of Lima who refused to permit the continued publication of *La Razón* on the chancery press. Leguía shrewdly followed the freeing of the labor leaders with an edict closing *La Razón* permanently.

During the labor unrest the workers also had the active support of the university students and their organization. Since the turn of the century there had been ferment in most Latin American universities. This unrest centered around student dissatisfaction with the traditional methods of instruction, the rote learning, and the pervasive neo-scholastic academism that stifled free inquiry. In 1919 students at the University of Córdoba in Argentina, openly revolted against the university administration. The spirit of revolt quickly spread throughout Latin America. In Lima a four-month student strike coincided with the labor unrest. Following a long tradition of sympathy for the cause of the workers, the students joined, and in some instances actually led, the street demonstrations. Student participation in labor's struggle for higher wages and shorter hours served to demonstrate their dissatisfaction with an educational system that totally ignored Peru's social and political problems. Mariátegui at once supported the students in their demands for university reforms. He saw the student reform movement as an expression of increasing intellectual concern for social and political questions. The task was to turn that along a socialist path.[17]

President Leguía attempted to drive a wedge between the students and workers. While freeing the labor leaders, he simultaneously cracked down on the students, jailing their leaders Victor Raúl Haya de la Torre, Luis Alberto Sánchez, and Manuel Seoane. The edict closing *La Razón* was part of this overall strategy of depriving the workers of any intellectual guidance and support. During the student-labor demonstrations, the student leaders had opened schools for workers called Popular Universities of González Prada. Their aim was to educate the workers politically, and to get them to organize as a political movement under student leadership. Leguía promptly outlawed the Popular Universities. This had the effect of driving Mariátegui and the students into close association—an association that had been heretofore non-existent. Thus began the political and personal friendship of Mariátegui and the promising young student leader, Haya de la Torre. This friendship would later founder due to an ideological schism, but not before each learned something from the other—Haya de la Torre, the basic theory of indigenous nationalism that guided his own organization, and Mariátegui the rudiments of organizing a political party in a hostile environment.[18]

The students and Mariátegui's group held many similar views due to the González Prada heritage in Peru. They believed that the intellectuals were the leaders of the social revolution which would inevitably come to their country. The two groups also saw the need to organize and to begin the task of educating the proletariat. Their organization would be a microcosm of the new society that they wanted to bring to Peru. Mariátegui in particular viewed this organization almost as a monastic order. Each individual would have to make a personal transformation in order to participate in the great revolutionary task of bringing socialism to Peru. Each person in effect, underwent the same kind of change or conversion that society itself had to undergo before socialism could come to pass.

The student movement in Peru followed a different course than elsewhere in Latin America, as for example Argentina and Venezuela. In Peru the students were violently suppressed, thus driving them to more extreme forms of action and making them bitter enemies of the Leguía regime. The students also were tied to the potentially explosive labor movement. Leguía had failed to split the students and workers, so he moved in another direction to gain more active support of the army and businessmen. The most extreme of the workers' demands were met with token reform measures.[19]

The importation of Chinese laborers had begun in the mid-nineteenth century. They replaced the slaves on plantations and were used in railroad construction. By 1919, many had settled in Lima and this visible minority was a key source of worker unrest. Leguía abruptly halted Chinese immigration in order to pacify the workers.[20]

Conciliatory on one front, Leguía moved firmly on another. He offered key student leaders, Mariátegui, and others of the *La Razón* group, the alternative of imprisonment or well-paid exile. Mariátegui was offered a minor diplomatic post in Italy, and "scholarship" for study in Europe. He faced the choice of risking his position in Peru as head of nascent socialist movement or of languishing in prison, which in his state of health would certainly have meant an early death. Mariátegui decided to take the proferred "scholarship." Throughout his career he would have to defend that decision, for he had compromised a "principle."[21] Whatever his reasons for acceptance, the European sojourn was a decisive turning point in his life. In Europe he would finally lay the religious problem to rest. His search for the meaning and purpose of life would end in his conversion to the doctrine of revolutionary Marxism. Through Marx, God would become one with Man, and the world would acquire a "new" meaning for the young man who rejected the religion of his mother. The process of conversion to revolutionary Marxism was a complex one for Mariátegui. The pilgrimage began in France in 1919, and ended in Germany in 1923.

4

European Exile
1919-1923

Mariátegui, Falcón, and Félix del Valle left Peru in the closing months of 1919. In those days a trip to Europe meant a long sea voyage lasting anywhere from six weeks to two months. Yet travellers from the west coast of South America no longer had to debark at the Pacific side of the Isthmus of Panama, take a train to the Gulf port of Colón, and then board a ship for the Atlantic voyage. Mariátegui's ship steamed through the newly completed Panama Canal and the five-year-old engineering feat greatly impressed him. The powerful influence of the United States seemed everywhere. A later stop at New York City was an awe-inspiring experience for him. (Lima in Mariátegui's day had a population of around 500,000.) Later he would conclude that North America was the last and strongest bastion of capitalism, a bastion that would eventually fall before the emerging Marxist giant—the Soviet Union.[1]

The voyage terminated in France where the three exiles parted company. Mariátegui proceeded to Paris and settled in the Latin Quarter, a famous post-war haven for writers, artists, and intellectuals of all nationalities. The first days were spent sightseeing and trying to improve his very poor command of French. His residence in the Latin Quarter, a hot-bed of left-wing political activity, led to his meeting many young political activists and intellectuals. Mariátegui met Henri Barbusse, a leading figure among the left-wing Socialists and later a co-founder of the French Communist Party. Barbusse was an ascetic, mystical man who inspired his followers with a reverential respect. He was like a father to them and became so to Mariátegui. This quality was not unlike the aura that had surrounded the last Socialist leader Jean Juarès. But Barbusse differed greatly from the brilliant, saint-like Juarès in his interpretation of socialism. Since these ideas greatly influenced Mariátegui, it is necessary to outline the French Socialist Movement of the early twentieth century.

The Socialists in France had passed through a fiery period in the first two decades of the twentieth century. The great debates over whether the Socialists should or should not support France in the World War had irreparably splintered the movement. (Barbusse had held out for the latter position.) There was perhaps some hope for Socialist reunification, but the assassination of Juarès on the eve of the conflict removed the only figure capable of reuniting the Socialists again. Basically, all French Socialists believed in the ultimate goal of the abolition of private property, and the redistribution of material goods to provide everyone with enough to live. But what divided them was the formula for action to achieve that goal.

Barbusse and his followers held that the collapse of capitalism was inevitable, that it was an enemy to be destroyed. Others, who followed Juarès approached the question of achieving socialism quite differently. They saw that their success lay in gaining the support of the working class. But in order to do so they had to show some practical accomplishments to demonstrate their sincerity and effectiveness in representing that class. Yet every practical gain that bettered the worker's lot seemed to put off the day of proletarian revolution. (It is this issue that had divided the French Socialists since the 1899 Party Congress. There the Socialists had split into two groups—the Socialist Party of France under Jules Guesde and Marx's son-in-law Paul LaFarque, and the French Socialist Party under Jean Juarès and Aristide Briand.) The belief in revolution with its implicit threat of violence, was no longer the universal bond of the French Socialists. To Barbusse, the other socialists were

merely "possibilist" reformers who sought not the destruction
of the bourgeois state, but its capture. Juarès and his followers
were "revisionists" who had lost sight of the meaning of
orthodox socialism.[2]

Barbusse viewed the task of the revolutionaries as a moral
crusade. This task was none other than a complete destruction
of the decadent bourgeois state. The Great War signified to
him the final tragedy of the passing bourgeois-capitalist age—
an age which had so corrupted men and so dehumanized them
that they had engaged in the most savage bloodbath in human
history. Christianity, the great civilizing force of the West, had
failed the teachings of Christ by becoming an appendage of the
old order. Barbusse's interpretation of post-war Europe coincided almost exactly with Mariátegui's view of Peru, and from
their first meeting the two men were drawn to one another.
Mariátegui was profoundly impressed with the man's dedication, his asceticism, and his deep concern for all mankind.
Barbusse on the other hand, saw Mariátegui as ". . . a new
light of America, a new specimen of American man."[3]

Mariategui's conversion to the doctrine of revolutionary
Marxism began in France while he was listening to the lectures
of Barbusse. Barbusse was a leading exponent of a trend in
early twentieth century French thought which may be termed
"revolutionary pacifism." (Later, he abandoned this position
and became a professed Communist.) He violently opposed any
involvement in the Great War on both moral and political
grounds. In Barbusse's view, there was little difference between
the two. The resurgence of nationalist feeling among the workers in France had dealt a serious blow to his hopes for a proletarian uprising. The old bourgeois-capitalist order had under-
mined the moral character of man, and the war was the culmination of this degenerative process.

Barbusse's ideological picture of the world was his moral
code as well, and this is perhaps his major contribution to the
development of Mariátegui's thought. Mariátegui absorbed not

so much Barbusse's ideas, as he did his mentor's way of look-
ing at the world and interpreting it. The tendency to view the
world in universal political-religious terms was already present
in Mariátegui's make-up. Barbusse strongly reinforced that
tendency.

Barbusse believed that all men were brothers, even though
they did not recognize that fact.[4] Man's social condition was
one in which exploitation and violence prevailed. Society had
set man against man in a senseless quest for material gain. The
meaning of man's existence therefore, lay in his society. Man
could only be redeemed from his present state of depravity
through social and political action. *Life* was all important, not
death or a life hereafter. When construed in these terms, political activity became the highest sort of calling. It acquired a
mystical, redemptive quality. Both Barbusse and Mariátegui
interpreted the socialist society of Marx as a moral community
in which all men shared the material benefits of that society. In
such a society, man could realize himself and reach new heights
of achievement through collective activity. Basically, Barbusse
and Mariátegui were seeking a form of medieval corporate
community in which all men had reciprocal rights and responsibilities.

Barbusse was primarily concerned with the "dehumanization" of man by the modern social system, a system which
alienated man from himself and his fellows. Marx had also
been concerned about this dehumanization process in the
increasingly complex industrializing society of Great Britain.
However, Barbusse arrived at his dehumanization idea inde-
pendently of Marx. (Marx's early writings, which contained
the bulk of his work on the alienation-dehumanization theme,
were not published until 1932.) Basically Barbusse viewed the
process of dehumanization in the following terms: Each man
was eager to live a life free of material want, so that he could
realize his desires in any way he chose. But he was constantly
thwarted by other men, who, because of the structure of exist-

ing social relationships were forced to exploit one another in order to survive. Barbusse asked the question: "What promise exists for man's future, and how is it related to the present?" Sounding like the Camus of the 1920's he answered: "Around us there is only one word . . . Nothing . . . . this does not signify our nothingness or our misfortune, but on the contrary, our realization, and our deification, since everything is within us."[5] Dehumanization, Barbusse insisted, was caused by the pattern of man's social relationships. And if man was to end this unnatural state, he must change the social system in order to achieve his unlimited potential for good.

Barbusse took a Hegelian position, stating that divinity resided in man, not some other-worldly God as interpreted by Christianity. Jesus, in Barbusse's scheme, was a universal symbol of the goodness of man. Christianity had deformed Jesus. For Barbusse God existed not outside man, but within each human being.[6] Christianity, by becoming a social and political institution of the corrupt existing order, had abdicated its civilizing and redemptive mission. Therefore, it had to be replaced by a new, more vital moral force which would guide men in their search for self-fulfillment. That force was socialism.

Barbusse was not alone in developing this line of reasoning. It had been a major theme in nineteenth century European thought. His basic position can perhaps be summed up in a statement by a Frenchman who dealt with the same theme, André Gide (1895–1951) who wrote: ". . . if the Church had fulfilled the teachings of Christ there would be no need for communism . . . indeed the social problem would not exist at all."[7]

Barbusse and Mariátegui came to ask the same basic questions, and they saw the answers in society at large. The problems which the individual faced were rooted in the social system, not the individual. Barbusse eventually decided that the way to change the social system was through the application of the Bolshevik technique of seizing power. Mariátegui never went quite that far in accepting this form of political activity. His strategy was more of a missionary's proselytizing endeavor. It was not a pragmatically conceived, conspiratorial effort to forcibly change the social system through the capture and subsequent destruction of the machinery of government.

In 1919 Barbusse wrote a small treatise entitled *Clarté* (Clarity). Here he stated his views on the role of the intellectual in the making of a revolution.[8] Like González Prada, Barbusse believed that the masses had to be made aware of their historic mission. That historic mission was to be explained and *clarified* so that the masses could be mobilized. Hence the title *Clarté*. The *Clarté* group in France (and the *Claridad* group which Mariátegui later founded in Peru) were to educate the working class politically and culturally. The function of art and literature was political and moral, not merely ascetic as in decadent bourgeois society. To the Marxist intellectual the political and moral were the same thing. Thus the Marxist intellectual could hasten the day of the revolution by creating a cultural milieu that would spread revolutionary Marxist ideas.

This was the *Clarté* concept which became a fixed star in Mariátegui's revolutionary vision. The concept, however, had another interesting aspect which closely paralleled an idea of González Prada. This was that that *all* intellectuals were "free spirits" who could play a revolutionary role even though they were not fully converted to Marxism. Coinciding with the appearance of *Clarté* was the founding of Barbusse's "International of Thought," which was dedicated to the "Conquest of Thought" and the creation of a world proletarian culture.

For Barbusse and Mariátegui, the attitude of intellectuals in the making of revolution was primarily a spiritual and psychological one. It was to be an act of faith that would make men revolutionaries; all men would be bound together in the struggle. This struggle would give them a sense of identity and purpose that was now lacking in bourgeois-capitalist society.

Barbusse expanded this idea in *Le Couteau entre les Dents* (With the Knife Between the Teeth). He exhorted intellectuals to recognize their historic, redemptive mission of leading the masses to the revolution.[9] Here we see that as late as 1921 Barbusse was still imbued with the nineteenth century idea of socialism. The work of achieving socialism was to be a way of life for the revolutionaries (an idea that Mariátegui had as well). Barbusse spoke of the heroic age that existed after the Bolshevik Revolution and he introduced the idea that revolution, based on the Bolshevik model, was a creative endeavor rather than a destructive act.

The creativity of revolutionary activity, in Barbusse's view, was tied to the existential question of the purpose of man's existence. Everything existed within man and since men cannot predict the future, the sole purpose of life was to better man's existence through social and political action.[10] Man's highest form of creative power lay in his ability to create a social system that would enable him to realize his own potential for good (though this good was never clearly spelled out by Barbusse). Existing political and social institutions were absurd, since they were based on the rule of a minority over a majority. He believed that a "general interest" existed which was being suppressed by a "Particular Interest"—namely the bourgeois-capitalist order. This general interest that Barbusse spoke of, was basically an anti-rational, anti-scientific reaction to the dilemma of social change and the problems of the post-war world. He grandly defined the general interest as being, ". . . a scientific generalization of the maximum expansion of the individual."[11]

Science, according to Barbusse's anti-rational views, had eliminated all the mysticism in life. Thus the process of the total dehumanization and alienation of man was complete. "All is reduced to primary causes, and the essence of being is now under a research plan."[12] Rationalism and individualism, as represented by the bourgeois-capitalist order, were locked in mortal combat with anti-rational, collective forces of socialism. That combat could only be resolved in favor of the socialist revolutionaries. This was an inevitable fact because *they* possessed the stronger "myth" i.e., sense of man's moral purpose. This view of Barbusse's was accepted entirely by Mariátegui who wrote later:

> The ideal of our epoch . . . The new revolutionary order, will rationalize and humanize customs. It will resolve the problems that, due to its structure and function, the bourgeois order is powerless to resolve. It will consent to the freeing of women from domestic servitude, will assure the social education of our children, free matrimony from economic preoccupations. Socialism . . . accused of materialism, results finally from this point of view in a just demand for, and a renaissance of, spiritual and moral values oppressed by capitalist organization and methods. If ambitious and materialist interests prevailed in the capitalist epoch, the proletarian epoch, in its character and institutions, will inspire ethical interests and ideals.[13]

The months spent in Paris were perhaps the most important in the development of Mariátegui's thought. With Barbusse, he had developed a basic political and personal *weltanschaaung* which changed little over the succeeding years. This period was the high point in the development of Mariátegui's ideas. From that time on, Mariátegui's thought became a fixed pattern. That pattern of thought, for want of a better term, can best be called "romantic humanism." While he referred to himself as a Marxist "convicto y confeso" he also stated that: "I think that it is impossible to understand in one theory the entire panorama of the contemporary world. That it is not now possible above all, to fix in one theory, its movement."[14]

Another great influence on the course of Mariátegui's thought was the great Spanish philosopher and writer, Miguel de Unamuno y Jugo. Mariátegui became acquainted with him in France at about the same time he met Barbusse. He was so impressed by Unamuno that he began to devour his works enthusiastically.[15] The Spaniard was concerned with the same existential questions as Barbusse, but he approached them in a different manner. Unamuno never rejected Christianity outright as Barbusse had done. Nor did Mariátegui; probably due to Unamuno's influence. Unamuno maintained that Christianity had become institutionalized and he wanted to restore the vigor that had made it such a force for good in days of its persecution. Three of the Spanish philosopher's works are perhaps the most outstanding in this respect. In his book, *The Life of Don Quijote and Sancho,* he was concerned with the individual's quest for self-identity—for that unique quality which set one man apart from another. Don Quijote's seemingly futile search was interpreted as this quest for self-identity, which the old warrior did not achieve until his dying moments. Whispering to Sancho, Don Quijote dies happy saying, "At last I know who I am."

The Quijote theme of that search for identity and purpose was also presented in a less allegorical form in Unamuno's *On The Tragic Sense of Life* and *The Agony of Christianity.* Here Unamuno stated that the message of Christianity had been distorted by the Church. Christ did not come upon earth to bring men happiness. Rather, He came to bring mankind agony and struggle. Man's purpose in life lay in the earthly struggle against pain, adversity, and ultimate death. Only through struggle could man rise to achieve his sense of self-identity, his unlimited potential for good, and ultimately, eternal salvation. This idea had a profound effect on the young Mariátegui. He built his own personal political philosophy around the concept of the "agonic soul"; the man whose life is one of constant struggle against adversity, and whose glory was in the nobleness of the revolutionary struggle. The "agonic man" of Unamuno became the Marxist revolutionary in Mariátegui.

However, Mariátegui rejected any idea of an eternal salvation, just as he rejected any idea of a socialist millennial king-

dom on earth. Man had but one life, his earthly one. This life
had to be one of ceaseless struggle if man was to rise above the
dull treadmill that was human history. This was Mariátegui's
interpretation of the tragic sense of life.

> The messianic millennium will never come. Man arrives to
> leave once more . . . No revolution foresaw the revolution that
> would come afterward, although in its bowels it carried its seed.
> For Man, as the subject of history, nothing exists but his own
> personal reality. He is not interested in the abstract, but in the
> concrete struggle. The revolutionary proletariat lives in the
> reality of the final struggle. Humanity . . . lives the illusion of
> the final struggle.[16]

Mariátegui was always critical of Unamuno for interpreting
Marxism as a dull economic formula. He believed, as did
Barbusse, that the importance of Marx was the *spirit,* not the
letter of his philosophy.[17] While it is quite likely that Mariátegui experienced his early exposure to Marx through Henri
Barbusse, it was through Miguel de Unamuno that Mariátegui
resolved the religious dilemma that had been plaguing him for
almost ten years. Through Unamuno's idea of the "agonic
struggle" Mariátegui's life began to take on a new meaning.
Yet it was Barbusse who gave a sense of political direction to
that "agonic struggle." Through Barbusse and Unamuno,
Mariátegui began to develop his own interpretation of the revolutionary surge sweeping the world. More specifically, he began to develop a view of the course of social revolution in his
native Peru. This interpretation began to take shape during
his stay in Italy, the next stop on his European journey.

Mariátegui arrived in an Italy torn by governmental crises.
In the early 1920's the nation, like other European countries,
had experienced a sharp economic decline. The Socialists under Gabriele D'Annunzio came to power during this dark
period. Mariátegui arrived hoping to draw some valuable
practical lessons from the Socialists' exercise of power. He was

sadly disappointed. Through Valdelomar, Mariátegui had gained a favorable impression of the Italian Socialists' rule. D'Annunzio wanted to unite an Italy still very much splintered by the unification struggles of the late nineteenth century and the disasters of the Great War. Even though Italy was on the winning side in the war, the carnage of Caporetto and the mismanagement of the war led to much the same kind of soul-searching that had occurred in Peru after the War of the Pacific.

D'Annunzio hoped to build a mass following that would unite the Italian people. He relied primarily on the intellectuals to realize this task of spiritual unification. The Socialist leader had a blind faith in the ability of these intellectuals to create a new sense of purpose in the Italian people. Such faith was not borne out by subsequent events.

Mariátegui witnessed the fall of the D'Annunzian Socialists and the rise of Fascism during his stay in Italy. The failure of the Socialists was something he never forgot; and he vowed never to make the same mistakes that D'Annunzio had committed. Mariátegui believed that the seeds of Fascism had been sown by D'Annunzio himself.[18] It was D'Annunzio who sought to unify Italy by creating the dream of rebuilding the Roman Empire. This nationalistic fervor had backfired on the Socialists and led to their downfall. The basic weakness of these Socialists, thought Mariátegui, was their lack of political program based on a sound ideology. Nationalism alone was not enough to sustain them.[19]

It was Mariátegui's view that the Italian Socialists had committed one blunder after another. They had tried to exercise power without a sound program, i.e. without an ideology. They had relied on the intellectuals and the bourgeois middle-class—the most rootless and disrupted elements in post-war Italy. They had completely ignored the urban and rural masses, and did not attempt to mobilize them until *after* they had attained power. The reliance on the emotion of nationalism led to their movement's capture by their greatest enemy—reaction in the form of Fascism.

Benito Mussolini, a former Socialist himself, had no illusions about intellectuals leading Italy—though he astutely used them for his own purposes. He even absorbed D'Annunzio into his Fascist Party. According to Mariátegui, the success of Mussolini's power-grab was due to his political astuteness, and that anti-revolutionary force—nationalism.

> Mussolini did not give a spirit, a program to fascism. On the contrary, fascism gave its spirit to Mussolini. . . . Mussolini had to assimilate, to absorb the anti-socialism, the chauvinism of the middle-class in order to enclose, and to organize this class into the ranks of the *fasci di combatimento*.[20]

Yet just as D'Annunzio had fallen, Mariátegui believed Mussolini would also inevitably fall, for Mussolini relied heavily upon the middle-class. The Fascists were merely a transitory phenomenon seeking to restore the old status quo that had been shattered by World War I and the Bolshevik Revolution. The period of reaction to socialism had set in. But Mariátegui had no doubt that the new ideology, socialism, would eventually triumph.[21] His observations of the Italian political scene convinced him of the necessity for building a sound ideology *before* attempting to found a political organization. Any doubts that he might have had in this respect were dispelled by D'Annunzio's downfall and Mussolini's triumph.

Mariátegui thought that the socialists should never compromise with the other so-called "non-revolutionary" classes, especially the bourgeoisie. Nor should they attempt to build a mass following based solely on nationalist appeals. He did not view nationalism per se as evil. Only when it became a vehicle of "reaction" i.e., of opposition to the socialists, was it a dangerous force. As Mariátegui saw it, the inherent danger of nationalism was the difficulty of controlling it once it had been unleashed. As an emotional appeal it was a useful tactic, but only if subject to the rigid ideological and organizational control of the revolutionary leadership. He never rejected the usefulness of nationalist sentiment, or of mass emotional appeals. But he considered them as tactics, not to be confused with ideology—the philosophical foundation of a political movement.[22]

Mariátegui did not spend all of his time in Italy observing D'Annunzian Socialism. He lived in Rome where he was a secretary to the Peruvian envoy, but his semi-official duties left him time for travel. He attended the Socialist Congresses in Genoa, Cannes, and Livorno as an observer. During these travels he met Anna Chiappe whom he finally married in Florence. This was the happiest time that he had known—his health was better due probably to the warm, sunny climate, and he had made peace with himself, found a life's cause and had married. This union endured through all the incredible hardships of the next nine years; and the beautiful Anna remained a source of love and inspiration throughout Mariátegui's lifetime.[23]

In 1922 their first child was born and was baptized Sandro in honor of Sandro Boticelli. Through Anna and her family, Mariátegui met Valdelomar's teacher Benedetto Croce. Mariátegui always regarded Croce as a leading "free thinker" of the Barbusse *Clarté* school, though Croce was never an ideological ally.[24] Following the birth of Sandro, Mariátegui laid plans for leaving Italy. He was anxious to see the rest of Europe before returning to Peru. Accompanied by his wife and son, he set out for the "second country of socialism"—Germany—stopping in Budapest to observe the effects of the 1919 Communist uprising, and then proceeding on to Vienna.

Many Marxists including Mariátegui believed that a revolutionary tide would sweep through Germany now that the Bolshevik Revolution had occurred. Germany of the 1920's had the largest and oldest Socialist party in Europe. The *Internationale* was sung by thousands of workers at party meetings, and the capital, Berlin, was called the "Red City of Western Europe." The situation appeared ripe for a socialist revolution in Germany; for the nation had suffered terribly after World War I. The economy was shattered, and rampant inflation had made the working class desperate.

Mariátegui wanted to view this impending struggle for socialism firsthand. He began feverishly to study German, but his poor command of the language hampered him throughout his six month stay in the country. César Falcón, who was living in Cologne, helped Mariátegui over the language barrier by travelling with him to Berlin and staying with the family there. Here the two men shared their experiences of life in European exile and planned their return to Peru.

Events in Germany convinced Mariátegui that the conclusions he had drawn from his Italian experience were more valid than ever. Germany of the 1920's was undergoing the same kinds of crisis that had shaken Italy. The Socialists, holding some 330 seats in the Bundestag were split into warring factions. The Social Democrats, who followed Karl Kautsky and Eduard Bernstein, were held in contempt by the militant Communists. They were viewed as traitors to the revolution since they had cooperated with the German state during the war. Mariátegui also thought that the Social Democratic approach to achieving socialism (i.e., the commitment to working through existing political institutions) was the same kind of "possibilism" that led to the downfall of the Italian Socialists.[25]

The Socialists, by compromising with other political groups, had played into the hands of the forces of reaction. The defeat of the Communist *Spartakusbund* movement in its bid for power, and the subsequent death of Wilhelm Liebknicht ended the hope that Germany would be the scene of the next socialist revolution. Mariátegui, somewhat disheartened by the turn of events, had met Maxim Gorky in Germany; and he decided that a trip to the Soviet Union would be a useful experience.[26]

However, the lack of funds, the chaotic internal situation in the U.S.S.R., and the opposition of his strong-willed wife who was expecting their second child prevented him from making the trip. In January of 1923 he bade farewell to Falcón, and began the three month journey back to Peru.

Before attempting to put his newly acquired revolutionary ideas into action, Mariátegui first had to re-acquaint himself with Peru and assess its revolutionary potential. He believed that the revolutionaries should *never* compromise with the forces of reaction as represented by the Leguía regime. This would only lead to the movement's capture by fascist reactionaries. He thought that the forces of reaction were on the march throughout the world. The socialist revolution would therefore be delayed for an indefinite period—at least until the collapse of fascism.[27] Mariátegui returned to Peru convinced that he must mobilize the intellectuals as the nucleus of his movement, and he followed the same approach as his mentor Henri Barbusse. He wanted to found a journal of ideological definition so as to mobilize the intellectuals. The publications that took up this task were *Claridad* (1923 and 1924), followed by the famous *Amauta* (1926-1930).

Mariátegui also wanted to simultaneously mobilize the urban workers. Drawing upon his Italian experience, he thought that this task could be started immediately. It would take some time to convince the workers of their revolutionary destiny—to develop a sense of class consciousness. Ultimately, Mariátegui thought that it would be necessary to organize a political party. This party was to be open to all who wanted to change Peru's social system. Significantly, actual control of the party was to be in the hands of a small nucleus of dedicated Marxist revolutionaries. This formation of a political party was to follow the development of a program of ideological definition. Mariátegui was extremely hesitant to commit himself to political action without having first laid the ideological groundwork.

This hesitancy to organize a political party can be best ex-

plained in the light of Mariátegui's Italian experience and his
Marxist view of the world. He viewed the revolutionary struggle as one that extended beyond the borders of Peru, and even
beyond his lifetime. As he saw it, his role was to begin the
"agonic" struggle in Peru. But first Mariátegui, like Marx, had
to discover the existing revolutionary forces in his society. At
this stage of his career he was not overly concerned about
organizing these revolutionary forces into a political party.
His goal, the establishment of socialism in Peru, still needed an
operational blueprint.

In 1923 Mariátegui's view of a socialist society was that of a
form of social relationships that would provide social and material equality for all men. This was as much a product of Marx
as it was of the glorification of the Inca heritage in Peruvian
thought. In order to achieve this socialism, Mariátegui believed
that every aspect of the existing social structure in Peru either
had to be changed or destroyed.[28] This was particularly true of
the system of land ownership, the hacienda system and landed
aristocracy. Mariátegui held that economic power conferred
political power and he was not of the view that the land tenure
system could ever be reformed. The landed aristocracy held the
Peruvian economy in its grasp and would not voluntarily give
up its dominant position. Therefore it had to be destroyed.[29]

Mariátegui believed that the "myth", the belief in the system
of democracy, still had a powerful influence on men. But this
democratic "myth" would be overcome by the socialist "myth"
which was gradually absorbing all of the spiritual élan that
democracy had possessed. History was on the side of the socialists since they had discovered the "historical truth" of their
age. They would inevitably succeed in their attempts to establish a new society. They had found the "truth" that was relevant for their age. In this respect Mariátegui wrote: ". . . the
truth of today will not be the truth of tomorrow. A truth is
valid only for an epoch. We must content ourselves with a relative truth.[30] For Mariátegui, that relative truth was socialism.

Mariátegui did not return from Europe laden with millennial dreams. He did not believe that socialism was some utopian state that could end all of man's problems. Rather, socialism was the next stage of man's inexorable march through history. History proceeded dialectically through epochs or stages of development. These stages were punctuated by intellectual and political struggle. This struggle which sometimes brought on violence, was the process by which one social order replaced another in endless succession. Each stage was a step in man's discovery of himself and his potential for good. He believed that he had discovered himself, *and* America while in Europe. Now Mariátegui wanted Peruvians to discover Peru.

> Europe [he wrote] revealed itself to me . . . as a primitive and chaotic world. At the same time it impelled me, and clarified for me the necessity of an American task. . . . Europe, for the American as for the Asiatic, is not only in danger of denationalization and dislocation, it offers the greatest possibility for the recovery, and discovery of one's own world, and destiny.[31]

Mariátegui believed that his task was a heroic one. Yet if he had indeed "discovered" America and Peru, the problem remained how to conquer it for socialism. He viewed that conquest in the following context:

> The renaissance, liberal myth has grown too old. The proletariat has a myth; social revolution. It moves toward this myth with a relevant, active faith. The bourgeoisie denies, the proletariat affirms. . . . The strength of the revolutionaries lies not in the science; it is in their faith, in their passion, in their will. It is a religious, mystical, spiritual strength. It is the emotion of myth. . . . The revolutionary emotion . . . is a religious emotion.[32]

Imbued with this "new faith," Mariátegui began to lay the groundwork for the socialist revolution in Peru.

5

THE YEARS OF HOPE
1923–1926

Mariátegui arrived in Peru in March of 1923, determined to begin the "heroic" task of building a Peruvian Marxist revolutionary movement. But he found that the complexion of the political situation had changed during his three year absence. Militant students and intellectuals had united in their opposition to the regime of Augusto B. Leguía. This opposition was organized under the leadership of Victor Raúl Haya de la Torre, one of the leaders of the student revolt of 1919 who had emerged as the leading figure in the protest movement. At the time of Mariátegui's arrival in Peru, this movement was one of protest only. It had no clear-cut goals, program, or ideological foundation.

Haya de la Torre had become the undisputed leader of the militant students and intellectuals in the early 1920's. He had taken the lead in attacking Leguía, and had cemented the ties between the students and workers that had been forged in 1919. Mariátegui had known Haya before his exile, but they had never been close friends. Soon, however, the two men were drawn together in a loose association that opposed the dictator Leguía.

Mariátegui spent the first few months in Lima contacting old friends and potential allies. On one occasion while in the offices of the newspaper *El Tiempo,* he met Haya de la Torre. At that time Haya asked Mariátegui if he would lend his support to a movement that was protesting the proposed consecration of Peru to the Sacred Heart of Jesus.[1] Mariátegui stated that while he was basically in agreement with the protest, he would not actively support it. He differed ideologically with Haya and believed that Haya had no sense of political direction, no ideology. The planned protests he thought, were merely a part of, ". . . a liberalizing struggle, without any revolutionary sentiment."[2]

There was no doubt that Mariátegui was in a basic disagreement with Haya de la Torre over the objectives and strategy of a Peruvian revolutionary movement. He was determined to form an alliance of "free spirits," but he refused to submit to anyone else's leadership. Unlike Haya de la Torre he could never be a pragmatist who could constantly adjust his tactics to fit a changing political situation. For Mariátegui, the building of a revolutionary movement based on an uncompromising ideology was his own "heroic" task, his *personal* mission in life. He was not about to surrender that role.

> In truth [he wrote] I am not sure that I have changed . . . [due to his European experience]. . . . I have matured more than changed . . . on my way I have found a faith. But I found it early, for my soul had left in search of God. I am an agonic soul as Unamuno would say. . . . Some years ago I had written that I had no other ambition than to realize my own personality. Now I would rather say that I only want to fulfill my destiny. Actually this is saying the same thing.[3]

Haya went ahead with the organization of the protest demonstrations without Mariátegui's support and on May 23, 1923, a series of strikes and street demonstrations broke out. The police moved quickly to break up the disturbances, killing a worker and a student in the process. Almost immediately after this incident, Mariátegui joined with Haya in opposing the proposed consecration, and more importantly the Leguía regime in general. It is not clear why Mariátegui made such an about-face, but there are two possible explanations. He perhaps realized that he could further his own ends by taking advantage of the existing political organization that Haya de la Torre had built up during Mariátegui's enforced exile. Another explanation is that he was deeply shocked by the brutal police suppression of the demonstrations, and felt that he could not remain silent in the face of such brutality. Quite possibly he was motivated by both of these factors.

Whatever his reasons, Mariátegui now became an ally of Haya de la Torre and part of Haya's organization, the Frente Único de Trabajadores Manuales e Intelectuales (The Only Front of Manual Workers and Intellectuals). Haya was apparently impressed with Mariátegui's dedication, and quite likely with some of his ideas as well. In 1923 he and Mariátegui founded *Claridad,* which was to be a journal of intellectual mobilization. It was directed by Haya, but Mariátegui, who had newspaper experience, was the managing editor. It soon became evident that the two men did not work together in complete harmony.

Actually, the instruments and institutions in which Mariátegui and Haya de la Torre made common cause were used to advance their own separate purposes. Mariátegui wanted to use the elements that Haya had mobilized to build a movement that was consistent with his own ideas on revolution. (The organizations that developed were: The Federation of Peruvian Students, The Popular Universities, and the journal *Claridad.*) Haya, on the other hand, probably wanted to take advantage of Mariátegui's prestige, his journalistic experience, and his theoretical ability. Quite possibly, he also wanted to neutralize a potentially dangerous political rival.

In addition to being actively engaged in directing *Claridad,* Mariátegui participated in the program at the Popular Universities (Universidades Populares de González Prada), These Universities were evening schools founded in the major cities of Peru, and they were staffed by students from the Federation of Peruvian Students. Their purpose was to bring "culture" to the workers, and to channel their political energies into Haya's movement. Mariátegui probably distrusted the Student Federation and the Popular University Movement, even though he supported them. He still had a basic distrust of intellectuals in general, since most of them were from the upper class and were products of a "feudalistic" educational system. Yet the Popular Universities were a means of contacting the semi-literate proletarians who were beyond the reach of his pen. Mariátegui's addresses to the workers in Lima had the sole purpose of, ". . . creating a sense of class consciousness and a knowledge of their historic mission . . . as the vanguard of revolution."[4]

Mariátegui had apparently convinced Haya de la Torre of the utility of the *Clarté* concept, as the journal *Claridad's* content indicates. Significantly, beginning with the fifth number the orientation of *Claridad* shifted. Instead of appealing solely to students and militant intellectuals, it also attempted to reach the workers as well.[5] The journal became affiliated with the newly organized Local Workers' Federation. Mariátegui often appeared at the workers' gatherings to deliver his editorials and essays in person. These speeches dealt mostly with his European experiences, the situation in Europe, and his view of world revolutionary trends.[6]

Compared to the charisma that Haya de la Torre exuded, Mariátegui cut a dull figure on the speaker's platform. Small in stature, frail in appearance, and possessing a thin, squeaky voice, Mariátegui's falsetto-like delivery did not inspire the proletarians to great heights of revolutionary fervor. His forte, as he well knew, was in his ability as a writer. His strength was in his pen, where his fervor and dedication stood out from the often illogical content of his articles.

Nowhere was Mariátegui's ability as an essayist more demonstrated than in his *Claridad* articles. Here he made his first attempts to develop an ideological foundation for his Peruvian Socialist Revolution. He wrote that *Claridad* was founded to:

> . . . fulfill the admirable invocation of the International of Thought, and to make the revolution of spirits. It rejects . . .

the predominate complicity in bourgeois reporting that silences
or falsifies the truth of this transcendent hour of the world, in
which the historic coming of a more beautiful and profound
spirit of social justice will be implanted in the conscience of all
men. . . ."[7]

This stirring rhetoric began to attract a growing number of
intellectuals. However, the Leguía regime saw his essays in a
more mundane light. *Claridad* was viewed as a dangerous
opposition organ and promptly closed down by the police.
Mariátegui immediately protested this action in a letter to the
editor of the newspaper, *La Crónica*. He stated, "*Claridad* is
not an oppositionist organ, but a reflection of a vast, world-
wide ideological movement. . . . *Claridad* is very far from the
sordid interests that are able to instigate a *coup d'etat* in this
epoch. It is . . . . a means of socialist ideology."[8] Clearly Mariátegui did not view his revolutionary essays as a threat to Leguía. His view of revolution was a long-range one. Yet to
Leguía, Mariátegui was preaching revolution and this was
intolerable.

The police, however, did not interfere with the Popular
Universities where Mariátegui gave some seventeen lectures in
1923 and 1924.[9] In these lectures he tried to explain the meaning of the world revolutionary surge and the dream of the "proletarian conquest of culture."[10] Actually, Mariategui's only
real tie with the workers came from his earlier defense of them
in the 1919 strikes. It was through Haya de la Torre and his
Frente Único, that Mariátegui renewed and strengthened his
connections with this class.

In October, 1923, Leguía finally moved against the Frente
Único. The police arrested Haya de la Torre, provoking mass
demonstrations by students, the Workers' Federation of Lima,
and the Textile Workers' Unions. Mariátegui joined in the
protests and participated in a planning session to map out further action. The meeting, which attracted about fifty persons,
was raided by the police and all the participants were jailed.

Some days later most of the group was released and Haya de la Torre was sent into exile. The leadership of the Frente was then delegated to Mariátegui with Haya retaining titular control from abroad.

The constant activity of demonstrations, editing *Claridad*, and writing for the militant trade union journal *El Obrero Textile* taxed Mariátegui's delicate health. This intense pace finally resulted in his complete collapse in the spring of 1924. He developed a high fever, and was rushed to Lima's Italian Hospital. There doctors discovered that his troublesome left knee had become so infected that amputation was necessary if his life were to be saved.

Despite the objections of his mother, Mariátegui's wife consented to the operation. Later, when Mariátegui discovered that he had lost his leg and would be an invalid for the rest of his life, he became completely unhinged and screamed for a quick, merciful death.[11] The experience was a turning point in his life. From that time on his condition would not permit him to take part in the intense physical activity so necessary to build his movement. That would have to be done by others. He was to be surrounded by his wife and a small band of faithful associates, who as time passed increasingly influenced his judgment.

In one aspect Mariátegui's illness worked in his favor. Throughout 1924 Leguía's police were busy rounding up and deporting opposition leaders *en masse*. The leaders of the students and workers all fell victim to the authorities. By the end of 1924, Mariátegui was the most prominent opposition leader left in Peru. Apparently Leguía thought that Mariátegui could not pose much of a threat as he was now an invalid with an advancing tubercular condition that would not permit him to live more than a few short years. The dictator had underestimated his adversary.

In the fall of 1924, after a brief period of convalescence, Mariátegui immediately took up the struggle once more. He wrote a letter in *Claridad* (which Leguía had permitted to reopen), on the effects of his recent illness and the present state of the world revolutionary movement.

> I want to defend myself from all sad influence and melancholy suggestion. And I feel more than ever the necessity of our common faith. . . . Our cause is the great human cause. . . . The world-wide perspective is more comforting than yesterday. Reaction retreats, conquered in the larger countries of the world. . . . In Germany the nationalist and reactionary current declines, and her martial caudillos have lost. [A reference here to the failure of the Hitler-Ludendorff putsch.] Fascism in Italy is also decomposing. The reactionary method has failed everywhere. The capitalist regime has found itself constrained to accept peaceful coexistence with the communist regime. . . . Let us obey the voice of History, and prepare ourselves to occupy our place in history. . . . Unequivocal signs announce that the future belongs to the revolution.[12]

This statement was the first indication that Mariátegui had revised his revolutionary timetable. This might have been due to the turn of world events. But more likely it was due to his realization that he had but a few years to live. If he wanted to ensure the success of a socialist revolution in Peru, he would have to lay the groundwork quickly. No longer could he afford the apparent luxury of postponing the organization of his *own* movement until he had developed a full-blown ideology. Organization and ideological development would have to proceed simultaneously. From this time on, Mariátegui pursued these two ends.

While Mariátegui resumed his activity in Peru, Haya de la Torre had not been idle. In Mexico, Haya founded the Alianza Popular Revolucionaria Americana (The American Popular Revolutionary Alliance, or APRA as it is commonly called). The founding of this new organization in May of 1924 was accompanied by Haya's declaration of the hemispheric alliance of workers, militant intellectuals, and students. This alliance was intended to bring about basic social and economic change throughout the hemisphere. Mariátegui never formally joined APRA, but did view it as consistent with his own objectives. He therefore gave tacit support to the nascent organization, perhaps hoping that it could be an excellent front that he himself could utilize.

The idea that a social revolution could be brought about by a grand alliance of all "free spirits" was expressed in the APRA program, and Mariátegui fully agreed with this. In Peru, the alliance was loose; and Mariátegui was free to pursue his own objectives within the organizational structure. (APRA did not emerge as a political party in Peru until 1928. It subsequently became known as the Partido Aprista Peruano [PAP].) While supporting APRA, Mariátegui went ahead with his own plans, thus undercutting the APRA organization and Haya de la Torre's influence. It was clear that at least two Marxist, revolutionary movements were developing in Peru. Each was seeking a political base among the same groups and each also utilized the same nationalist and Marxist arguments. The struggle between Haya and Mariátegui for leadership of the revolutionaries began in earnest with the founding of APRA in 1924.

As late as 1926 Mariátegui was still thinking in terms of a spontaneous revolution that would immediately change Peruvian society. In contrast, Haya de la Torre believed that the capture of political power was the single most important element in bringing about any social change. He did not believe in the idea of revolutionary spontaneity, and he wanted the revolution to take place in his own time. Moreover, he was convinced that he should lead it.[13] Yet until 1928 Mariátegui the mystic, and Haya the pragmatist, worked together in a loose "fraternal" alliance. But their paths were diverging as Haya sought political power, while Mariátegui ignored the quest for power in his search for an ideology.

This search for an ideology that would chart the course of the socialist revolution in Peru was conducted with an eye to

the course of world events. Mariátegui believed that Europe
had been on the verge of a socialist revolution just prior to
World War I. But that war had aroused a sense of nationalism
among the proletariat and the small concessions granted by the
bourgeoisie had distracted the proletariat from its revolutionary
task. After the war, the bourgeoisie began to revoke those concessions; state control of prices, wages, transportation, and
basic industries was ending now that the crisis was over. In
Mariátegui's view, this was a reactionary bourgeois "counter-
offensive" against the forces of socialism.

Mariátegui believed that the post-war "reaction" would
cause a polarization of classes once again which would cause all
proletarians to unite under the leadership of a new generation
of Marxist intellectuals. The bourgeoisie, by following the path
of reaction, would be the main instrument in healing the socialist schism.[14] Mariátegui made this position clear in an article
written for *Claridad,* which read like an excerpt from Spen-
gler's *Decline of the West* (1918), a book that had great impact
on the post-war generation in Europe.

> We are presiding over the death of historicism, of rational-
> ism, of the ideological bases of bourgeois society. Contemporary
> thought is saturated with relativism and skepticism, and this is
> transcendental. . . . A civilization in apogee produces a philos-
> ophy that is affirmative, constructive, and dogmatic. A negative,
> destructive, and skeptical philosophy on the other hand is the
> product of a declining, moribund civilization.[15]

It was this same view of the world that Mariátegui
attempted to convey in his speeches to the workers at the Popular University lectures. He argued that the potential for a
socialist revolution in Peru resulted from the creation of an
international civilization by the forces of capitalism. Capitalism
had created *material* ties among all peoples; but it had not
created any *spiritual* ones since it destroyed the existing spiritual bonds that had existed before the capitalist epoch. Capital-

ism, by its very nature, was capable only of destroying the spiritual ties of men, not of strengthening or creating those ties. Only socialism could perform this spiritual function so vital to men in an increasingly impersonal world.[16] Mariátegui rejected the "yellowism" of the Second International i.e., the decision by some socialists that socialism could be achieved in some cases through cooperation with the bourgeosie. Any compromise with bourgeois-capitalist regimes debilitated the zeal of the revolutionary forces, thus lessening the likelihood that a socialist revolution would take place.[17] Here, Mariátegui evidenced a logical contradiction common in the thought of many Marxian socialists. On the one hand, he spoke of inevitable revolution; yet on the other, he argued that the revolutionaries had to take advantage of the historical circumstances to make that revolution. They must never compromise their principles else the revolution would not occur.

The main thrust of Mariátegui's thought once he returned from Europe was his search for a "Peruvian reality." This reality was nothing more than a socialism that would conform to Peru's unique social and cultural heritage. He did not believe that the revolutionaries could wait for capitalism to develop in Peru. This was because the middle class had no conception of their "historic function" i.e., the building of capitalism. The outlook of this class was still feudal and colonial, which meant that they stood mid-way between capitalism and socialism. The middle class therefore had to be destroyed, and capitalism brought about by the socialists themselves. Socialism would, then, inevitably follow.[18]

Mariátegui argued that while Peru and Latin America were politically independent, they were actually colonial economic dependencies of the industrial powers. This economic dependency had a pervasive influence on every aspect of life, especially intellectual activity. Economic dependency coincided with intellectual dependency. There was no such thing as a Latin American thought; it was merely an imitation of Western

European ideas. He urged the intellectuals to engage in a dialogue, and to look to their own cultural heritage for their ideas. There they would discover their own unique "reality," and would thus make an original contribution to their country's cultural and social life.[19]

He attempted to apply his own dictum to Peru by examining its indigenous past as the possible key to its future course. He looked past the colonial period as if it never existed. The three-hundred-odd years of the colonial era were but an interlude that had interrupted Peru's "true" historical development. Mariátegui reinterpreted the social and economic institutions of the Incas and attempted to relate this indigenous heritage to his goal of achieving a modern socialist society.[20]

However, he did not believe that the Indians who had retained their native customs and traditions over the centuries could be the catalytic factors in his developing program for revolution. The indigenous peoples, and most inhabitants of the countryside in general, were essentially a passive and conservative people. Their long years of exploitation and suffering in a semi-feudal condition did not make them receptive to revolutionary ideas. The "true" revolutionary spirit resided in the cities. This spirit would spread to the countryside only after it had taken hold among militant urban intellectuals and workers. Mariátegui gave González Prada's thesis a Marxist twist when he wrote:

> . . . the revolutionary spirit . . . always resides in the cities, and this fact has clear and historic motives. It is in the city where capitalism has reached its fullness, and where there is freedom for the real battle between the individualist order and the socialist idea. . . . While the city educates man for collectivism, the countryside excited his individualism. . . . What distinguishes and separates the city from the countryside is not therefore revolution or reaction. It is above all a difference of mentality and spirit, which emanates from a difference of function.[21]

No explanation was provided for the fact that the "individualist" countryside had kept the corporate social structure of the Incas alive for some three centuries. Nor did Mariátegui ever explain what he meant by "a difference of function." He extolled the idea of "La América Indo-Española." Yet by doing so he raised the spectre of the nationalism which he had specifically condemned.[22] He was not interested in subtleties. He was engaged in articulating what he believed was the revolutionary mood of his time. His task as he saw it, was to fill a vacuum in Peruvian thought.

> In Peru, [he wrote] we have no similar teacher [like José Vasconcelos, Miguel de Unamuno, or José Ingenieros] with sufficient mental audacity to sum up the voices of our time, with sufficient apostolic temperament to affiliate himself with a renovative, combative ideology.[23]

The "renovative and combative" ideology which Mariátegui was striving to develop for Peru was a blend of Marxist and nationalist themes. We have already seen how he had become acquainted with Marxism while in Europe. But the nationalism in Mariátegui's thought (which will be examined in detail later) is more difficult to trace to a specific point of origin. Basically, Mariátegui drew upon indigenous themes in an attempt to link Peru's socialist future to its past history. He thought that any developing socialist society must take into account the rich heritage of the indigenous past. It was this heritage that was the basis for his concept of Peruvian "reality."

All elements of the social structure, and all political regimes that had grown up since the Conquest were viewed by Mariátegui as illegitimate since they did not take into account this indigenous heritage. Mariátegui's idealization of the Inca past was not original with him—this process had been a part of Peruvian thought since the late nineteenth century. Mariátegui was also influenced by his cultural anthropologist friend Luis

Valcárcel—the only one of Mariátegui's circle who had direct
experience with the indigenous peoples. The unique element in
Mariátegui's use of these indigenous themes was that he justified them on the basis of a Marxian analysis.

The indigenous, or nationalist element in Mariátegui's
thought can be summed up on one term—the myth of *Twantinsuyo*. Twantinsuyo was the Quechua term for the Inca
Empire of the pre-Conquest period. Literally, it means "land
of the four winds." The Inca Empire, this land of the four
winds, once extended from the present area of southern Ecuador, down the Andes to the Bolivian highlands, and through
what is now northern Chile. However, Twantinsuyo also signified a cultural, linguistic, and religious entity. Religion and
the state were inseparable. The head of state, the emperor,
was also the divinely anointed representative of the Sun-God
on earth. Within this society, all men had their tasks to fulfill;
each had his responsibilities for the functioning of the society.
But the society also was responsible for its citizens' moral and
material welfare. The corporate social structure which characterized Inca society was designed to meet those obligations.

This indigenous society was "rediscovered" during the soul-
searching that went on following the War of the Pacific.
Indeed, its "rediscovery" continues to the present day in Peru.
By Mariátegui's time, Twantinsuyo had become an idyllic state
of nature that Peruvian intellectuals longed for as an alternative to the existing order. For Mariátegui, Twantinsuyo was a
primitive form of socialism in which no man suffered material
want. Each was fed, housed, and clothed. More importantly,
each man had a purpose within that society, a sense of identity,
of belonging, and of loyalty to that society. Despite his protestations to the contrary, it was this latter element that Mariátegui sought to combine with the modern doctrine of Marxism.

In Mariátegui's writings the Black Legend of the Spanish
Conquest was revived with new vigor. The heritage of the
Conquest, and the republican era, was depicted as a mon-

strous evil that had to be destroyed. "The original sin" of the Conquest "was passed on to the Republic, of wanting to build a society and Peruvian economy without the Indian, and against the Indian."[24] This idealization of the Inca, and condemnation of the post-Conquest era served to inject an irrational, nationalistic element into Mariátegui's thought which could not be eliminated on the grounds of Marxist "science."[25]

Mariátegui's development of the Twantinsuyo myth posed serious problems. The existing social and economic structure was depicted as an *alien* system imposed on Peruvians by imperialist conquest. He sought to end this situation and rebuild Peru on the basis of its unique heritage of race, culture, and economic institutions. In reality, he was building a nationalist ideology of national integration, not an anti-nationalist one that conformed to the universal doctrine of revolutionary Marxism. It is quite likely that Mariátegui believed that he could control nationalist sentiment by subjecting it to the rigid ideology of Marxism. In 1925, when he first began to develop these indigenous themes, the Italian experience was still fresh in his mind. He justified the use of indigenous themes, which he acknowledged as being nationalistic, on the basis of his "scientific" Marxist analysis, not on the "sentimental" nationalistic grounds that had led to D'Annunzio's downfall.[26]

According to Mariátegui's Marxist-indigenous *weltanschaaung*, one could look at Peru and see the whole process of human history before him. The social structure of the existing order had all the elements of the historical process within it. It was bourgeois on the coast and feudal in the *sierra*. The corporate structure of the Inca society had been destroyed; but its traditions still remained deeply imbedded in the bewildered, and exploited Indian masses. This was the *real* tragedy of Peruvian history according to Mariátegui. The ruling classes were completely oblivious to "the value of human capital."[27] "The independence movements failed to create a new social and political entity because they were based on principles of the

French and American Revolutions . . . jacobin, bourgeois, and
liberal abstractions. They did not conform to the social reality
. . ."[28] i.e., Peru's cultural heritage.

Mariátegui did not view nationalism and socialism as incompatible elements in his revolutionary ideology. He believed that
socialism and nationalism were basically international phenomena. He wrote that the socialist idea, ". . . changes in these
peoples who are politically and economically colonial. Among
these peoples . . . socialism acquires by force of circumstances,
without renouncing any of its principles, a nationalist attitude."[29] His argument was that Peru (basically rural, agrarian, without a large urban proletariat, and with some two-thirds of its total population largely outside the modern sector
of society) must seek its own unique revolutionary path. A
sense of national identity had to be created in Peru before any
sense of international solidarity with the oppressed peoples of
the world could take place. National integration, therefore, was
the first objective in the building of Peruvian socialism.

> One of the most interesting phenomena, and one of the most
> extensive movements of this epoch is precisely this revolutionary
> nationalism, this revolutionary patriotism. The idea of the
> nation . . . is the incarnation of the spirit of liberty . . . and in
> Peru, those of us who represent and interpret peruanidad, the
> national identity, are those who in accepting it as an affirmation and not as a negation, work to give again a country to
> those who have been conquered and subjugated by the Spaniards, who have lost it for four centuries, and who still have not
> regained it.[30]

According to Mariátegui, the establishment of a national
identity based on race, culture, and social structure of the Incas
could only be achieved through revolutionary Marxism. The
solution to Peru's problems was economic, and this was where
Marxism played its role in Mariátegui's thought. He thought
that the economic structure had to be changed. All other social

and political changes would therefore follow. According to this view the Peruvian economy was still basically an export economy, and therefore still feudal and colonial.[31] How to bring about this economic change was a crucial question for Mariátegui. Once he had "discovered" the indigenous revolutionary forces in Peru, he was then faced with the problem of how to *make* that revolution. The theory of revolution had to be made operational. Mariátegui saw Peru as a society in stagnation, neither moving toward capitalism nor reverting to feudalism; it was stuck on dead-center, halfway between the two. His task, as he saw it, was to get Peru moving toward socialism and the first step in this "heroic task" was the founding of the journal *Amauta* in 1926.

6

Amauta
Journal of Revolution

The dream of founding a journal that would pave the way for the socialist revolution in Peru still posessed Mariátegui some three years after his return from Europe. *Claridad* had been an interim step, allowing him to reorient himself in Peru after his long absence. However, he did not found a *Clarté*-like journal immediately after returning from Europe due to poor health. He himself spoke of these "painful vicissitudes" that delayed this work.[1]

Despite poor health, Mariátegui was extremely active. Indeed, he seemed to be at physical peak during these years. It is true that he was penniless, and that his health was deteriorating gradually, but his activities were not curtailed because of this. Actually, Mariátegui was not a very organized person; it seems quite likely that procrastination was ingrained in his make-up. Mariátegui himself left a vivid description of his unsystematic work habits.

> I don't always work in the same way [he wrote the year he founded *Amauta*]. I adapt my work to my changing physical condition. . . . I always write at the last minute when I have to hand my articles to the printer. This habit is no doubt left over from my newspaper days. I have always written on a typewriter. But during my convalescence the typewriter tired me out. . . . Sometimes I dictate; other times I hand in horrible copy to the typist. I am concerned with method, and detest verbosity. . . .[2]

It is also quite likely that Mariátegui delayed the founding of his own revolutionary journal because he thought that *Claridad* would serve the same purpose. Mariátegui probably thought that he and Haya de la Torre could work effectively together. It was only when the two men began to drift apart that this journal *Amauta* made its appearance. As was usually the case with Mariátegui's publication ventures, he suffered from a lack of financial backing. Funds, however, seemed to be the least of his problems. Journals were founded with practically no capital in those days. (Indeed, when Mariátegui's publishing house, the Sociedad Editora Amauta was founded in 1926, it had a working capital of 7500 soles, or about $1400.00.)[3] Whatever Mariátegui's reasons for delaying the founding of *Amauta* until 1926, its appearance marked a growing split among the revolutionaries in Peru. When viewed in this perspective, the direction of Mariátegui's thought and the changing ideological position of *Amauta* from 1926 to 1930 form a pattern that can be analyzed.

By 1926, Mariátegui was convinced that his major rival, Haya de la Torre, was not on a truly revolutionary course. *Amauta* was founded because of the growing division between the various revolutionary factions. The increasing polemic forced Mariátegui to put forth an independent position and to found an organ that would represent that position. As the dispute became more heated during the 1920's, Mariátegui defined his ideological stance more sharply—it is this process of ideological definition that marks the course of *Amauta*.

Once Mariátegui had decided to start his own journal he gathered his followers together to plan its publication. A discussion followed as to what title it should bear. Some wanted to continue with *Claridad* in the Barbusse tradition while others argued for *Vanguardia.* Finally, the painter José Sabogal suggested the name *Amauta* and Mariátegui liked the idea. *Claridad* came too close to identification with Haya de la Torre's group; while *Vanguardia* sounded too much like the Vanguardista literary movement which Mariátegui viewed as decadent. *Amauta* however was altogether new, and it conveyed the idea of developing a uniquely *Peruvian* form of socialism. *Amauta* was a Quechua word that meant wise man. In the Inca Empire the *Amautas* were the sages—the advisers to the emperor. It was they who were the intellectual leaders of Inca society, responsible especially for the education of the prince before his accession to the father's throne.

Amauta was founded on the *Clarté* principle of the unity of all intellectuals in the great preparation for a spontaneous revolution. It did not openly support any political movement, especially APRA. Yet the journal was not an open forum for all shades of political opinion. Mariátegui's ideological position by 1926 was becoming harder and more inflexible and he clearly summed up that position in the first issue of *Amauta*. Interestingly, Mariátegui also defended his choice of the title *Amauta* in the same issue. He tried to distinguish his ideas from racist theories then in vogue by insisting that the choice of *Amauta* as a title was not due to any racist motives. It was instead, part of an attempt to direct attention to the rich heritage of the indigenous past which could be the foundation of the new Peruvian future. This opening essay in *Amauta* was one of the most cogent he ever penned; the translation appears below.

This journal in the intellectual field does not represent a group. Rather, it represents a movement, a spirit. For some time a current of change has been felt in Peru, vigorous and more defined each day. The supporters of this change are called *vanguardistas,* socialists, revolutionaries, etc. History has not given them a name yet. Among these groups there exist some formal discrepancies, some psychological differences. But above that which differentiates, is that which draws them together and unites them: their desire to create a new Peru in a new world. Gradually the understanding and coordination of the most willing of these elements progresses. The movement—intellectual and spiritual—takes shape little by little. With the appearance of *Amauta* it enters into a phase of definition.

Amauta has had a normal process of gestation. It is not born through any sudden determination that is exclusively mine. I came from Europe determined to found a journal, but painful vicissitudes did not permit me to fulfill this task. But this time has not passed in vain. My effort has been articulated with that of other artists and intellectuals who think and feel somewhat as I do. Two years ago this journal would have only been a personal voice. Now it is the voice of a movement, a generation.

The first effect that we, the writers of *Amauta* propose to achieve, is that our reaching an agreement and of getting to know ourselves better. The work of the journal will make us more as one. At the same time it will attract other good elements, and will separate the waiverers, the discouraged ones that now flirt with *vanguardismo;* but the latter movement hardly demands sacrifice from them, and they will hasten to leave it. *Amauta* will screen out the men of the vanguard—militants and sympathizers—even separating the chaff from the grain. It will produce, or precipitate a phenomenon of polarization and concentration.

It is not necessary to expressly state that *Amauta* is not a rostrum that is free and open to all winds of the spirit. We who found this journal do not conceive of an agnostic culture and art. We feel a belligerent, polemic force. We will not make any concession to the generally fallacious criterion of the tolerance of ideas. In the prologue of my book, *The Contemporary Scene,* I wrote that I am a man of doctrinal position [*filiación*], a faith. I can say the same thing of this journal, that it rejects all that is contrary to its ideology, just as that which has no ideology.

In presenting *Amauta* solemn words are not desired. I want to proscribe rhetoric from this journal. Programs seem absolutely useless to me. Peru is a country of labels and ceremonies. We are finally doing something with substance, that is to say with spirit. *Amauta* on the other hand needs no program; it needs only a destiny, an object.

The title will probably disturb some. This is due to the excessive, fundamental importance of a label among us. In this case one must not look at the strict meaning of the word. The title does not translate as our adherence to race, it does not merely reflect our homage to *incaísmo*. But with this journal the word *Amauta* takes on a specifically new meaning. We are going to create once more.

The object of this journal is to state, to clarify and become acquainted with the problems of Peru from doctrinal and scientific points of view. But we will always consider Peru within the world panorama. We will study all of the movements of social change [*renovación*]—political, philosophical, artistic, literary, and scientific. Everything human is within our scope. This journal will bind the new men of Peru, first with those peoples of Latin America, and finally with the other peoples of the world.

I will add nothing more. One will have to be shortsighted not to realize that at this moment, an historic journal is born to Peru.[4]

Amauta became an instant success among intellectuals throughout Latin America who saw it as a journal of their generation—a revolutionary generation. Most of the material was written by the Peruvian-based *Amauta* group. But articles and letters (some written expressly for *Amauta,* and some reprinted from other sources) written by Romain Rolland, Henrí Barbusse, Miguel de Unamuno, Rabindranath Tagore, and Soviet contributors gave the journal a unique international flavor.

Mariátegui and his group attempted to explore the range of the romantic, revolutionary period in which they lived. He himself commented extensively on the writings of this post-war generation in *Amauta's* review section. Perhaps one of the reasons for *Amauta's* wide appeal in Latin America was its treatment of new ideas, especially Marxist revolutionary ideas that were little known. For the Latin American intellectuals who wanted to change their respective societies, *Amauta* served as their means of communication with each other and with the revolutionary forces outside the hemisphere.

The stages of development of Mariátegui's thought in *Amauta* are roughly four in number: of the total of thirty-two issues that appeared from September 1926 to August 1930, some twenty-nine were published under his overall supervision. In this study, *Amauta* has been divided into the following categories for analysis: numbers 1 through 9—the period of ideological definition; numbers 10 through 16—the final schism of the left-wing revolutionary movement; numbers 17 through 29—the emergence of *Amauta* as an avowedly Marxist, socialist organ; finally, numbers 30 through 32 which appeared after Mariátegui's death (under the editorial direction of Ricardo Martínez de la Torre), and attempted to link Mariátegui with the communists. This approach is unlike that of most scholars who have studied *Amauta*—they have practically ignored the debate that raged among the left-wing intellectuals in the late 1920's. It is precisely this debate that is crucial to any understanding of the development of Mariátegui's thought and the ultimate collapse of his revolutionary movement after his death.[5]

The tone of *Amauta's* first stage was set by Mariátegui in the *presentación* cited above. As a journal of definition *Amauta* was open to anyone who believed in the necessity of uprooting the corrupt existing order. Haya de la Torre, Luis Alberto Sánchez, and other figures in the APRA movement were frequent contributors in these early issues. This fact did not pass unnoticed by Leguía's police. The participation of the APRA leaders gave the government cause to believe that *Amauta* was really a covert organ of the APRA, even though Mariátegui was careful not to affiliate himself with Haya's organization. Surprisingly, the new journal received a large amount of financial support in the form of advertising from the very organizations of "capitalist imperialism" that it was so vigorously condemning. The first nine issues were the most successful from a financial standpoint; large blocks of advertising were purchased by such firms as Pan American Grace, the Marconi Wireless

Company, Ford Motor Company, and foreign banks with branches in Lima. There is no available explanation for this paradox of "capitalist" support for Mariátegui's journal, but it is probable that the tolerance of the Leguía regime led to the placing of the advertising. Once that tolerance ended in June of 1927 advertising fell off sharply. The journal then led a precarious existence for the next three years.

The events that led to the closing of *Amauta* by Leguía and the arrest of Mariátegui and his followers are still obscure. It seems likely that Leguía was concerned about *Amauta's* connections with the APRA movement. Then, too, *Amauta* was attacking the very foundations of Leguía's government—foreign investors, large business interests, and the middle-class. Leguía thought that the germ of a communist revolution was being planted in Peru since *Amauta* attempted to draw analogies between the Bolshevik and Chinese Revolutions and the Peruvian situation. These analogies were actually highly distorted idealizations of the peasant and agrarian social structure in each country.[6] Mariátegui and his contributors had little direct knowledge of the course of the Chinese and Russian Revolutions, and perhaps even less of the lives of the peasant masses in Peru.

The main thrust of these first issues of *Amauta* consisted of an attack on the very foundations of the modern bourgeois state. The contributors were of one voice in decrying the decline of collective morality and the rise of a secularly oriented, impersonal social structure.[7] Mariátegui and his collaborators wanted to arrest, and finally reverse this process by defining an alternative path to modernization through socialism. This socialism, which would incorporate the uniquely Peruvian heritage of its indigenous culture into its program, was the new moral force that would end man's sense of isolation. It would give man a moral justification for his existence.[8]

In these early issues of *Amauta*, Mariátegui went to great lengths to avoid any discussion of differences between the revolutionaries. He still believed that the great work of revolution would be damaged by engaging in "byzantine" debates. Such debates merely hindered the process of ideological definition and needlessly split the intellectuals at a time when unity was of the utmost importance.

While *Amauta* engaged in the primary task of ideological definition, Mariátegui was also active in organizing the workers of Lima. In January, 1927 he addressed the First Workers' Congress in Lima. This marked his first attempt to organize the workers under his leadership, and undercut Haya de la Torre's influence. In his address Mariátegui explained his view of Marxism as it applied to Peru, and he spoke of the inevitable revolution that would come to his country. The address almost paralleled one given by González Prada to the workers of Lima some twenty-five years before. According to Mariátegui, the workers needed to develop a sense of class consciousness which was to be instilled in them by the "vanguard" (i.e., Mariátegui's group). The workers were "the proletariat of the vanguard" and were to "follow the heroic leadership" of the intellectuals. Echoing González Prada, Mariátegui stated that: "The mass always follows the same heroic, realistic, 'espiritus' creators." It was these "creators" that were to give the workers ". . . a realistic sense of history, and an heroic will of creation and realization."[9]

Following this address to the Workers' Congress the dispute between Mariátegui and Haya de la Torre burst into the open. Luis Alberto Sánchez, an old friend but devoted to Haya de la Torre, his colleague of student days, published an attack in *Mundial* on Mariátegui's ideological position. He stated that Mariátegui had not been faithful to the ideals put forth in the first issues of *Amauta*. Engaging in ideological definition did not seem to concern Sánchez who was concerned about Mariátegui's attempt to organize the workers. He viewed such an attempt as a clear threat to APRA and Haya de la Torre. Any rise of a revolutionary movement independent of APRA could

only weaken Haya's nascent organization in Peru. The Sánchez attack was obviously intended to weaken Mariategui's
position among the radical intellectuals and to hamper his
attempt to organize a separate movement.[10]

Mariátegui replied to Sánchez in *Amauta,* and a polemic
ensued between the two men in the February through April,
1927 issues of the journal. Sánchez attacked Mariátegui's
idealization of the Inca past and implied that it was merely a
façade to hide his "Europeanized" Marxist ideas; he accused
Mariátegui of attempting to foist an alien ideology upon Peru.
Mariátegui replied that his blend of indigenous and Marxist
socialism travelled the same path, and that each was inseparable from the other.[11] Mariátegui had always tried to avoid ideological disputes which, in his view, had been one of the primary reasons for the failure of the socialist revolutionaries in
Europe. Yet he had become embroiled in the kind of "byzantine" debate that he had vowed to avoid; Sánchez's remarks
could not go unanswered.

He tried to refute what was perhaps the most damaging of
Sánchez's charges—that he was an *"europeanizante"* (Europeanized intellectual who had lost touch with Peru). He argued that he was not trying to impose a foreign doctrine on
the Peruvian revolutionary situation. Mariátegui held that *his*
Marxism was "scientific" and that it conformed to the objective
conditions in Peru. He tried to demonstrate that unlike the
proletariat of Europe, the proletariat of Peru included the
Indian as well as the worker; therefore his Marxism had been
modified to fit the Peruvian context.

> Socialism [wrote Mariátegui replying to Sánchez] orders and
> defines the just demands [*reivindicaciones*] of the working class.
> And in Peru—the working class—are four fifths part Indian.
> Our socialism then, would not be Peruvian—it would not even
> be socialism—if it did not first consolidate itself with indigenous
> demands.[12]

In the continuing debate Luis Alberto Sánchez (who probably spoke for the exiled Haya de la Torre) accused the director of *Amauta* of being a dogmatist who attempted to stifle differences of opinion. Mariátegui replied by sidestepping the ideological issues that were posed; he accused Sánchez of engaging in an *ad hominem* argument, and stated that if Sánchez was going to call him anything let it simply be a socialist. In a denial that admitted his dogmatism Mariátegui stated, "There is no dogmatism in me. If there is it is a conviction, a passion, a fervor. I am a combatant, an agonic man."[13]

The revolutionary views of APRA and Mariátegui's group were both internationally oriented. Sánchez, however, tried to prove that Haya de la Torre and APRA were *more* internationally oriented than Mariátegui and his group. He accused Mariátegui of not being a soicalist at all, but merely a misguided nationalist. Worse yet, Mariátegui was a nationalist attempting to create a *nationalist* theory based on *alien* ideas. Mariátegui replied in the following note.

> Nationalism in Europe is apart from conservatism and imperialism. . . . But nationalism of the colonial peoples . . . is revolutionary, and therefore it travels the same path as socialism. In these peoples, the idea of the nation has not completed its journey, nor has it lost its historic mission. And this is not theory.[14]

The bitter dispute between the APRA forces and Mariátegui irreparably destroyed the Frente Único, and three separate revolutionary groups emerged from the Front: APRA led by Haya de la Torre, the Socialists led by Mariátegui, and a nucleus of Communists, which in 1928 existed *within* Mariátegui's group. Mariátegui had based his position on his own interpretation of Marxism and indigenous Inca socialism, but the empirical foundations of his ideology rested on the examples of the Bolshevik and Chinese Revolutions. Yet the power struggles among the Bolsheviks and Chinese seemed to seriously challenge the credibility of these revolutions as examples for Peru to follow.

He believed that the course of other revolutions in the world had a direct bearing on the Peruvian situation, and in particular he viewed the Mexican Revolution with dismay as the regime of Plutarco Elías Calles came to power. Revolutionary momentum was on the wane in Mexico, and the Thermidorian process of bureaucratization and institutionalization was beginning to set in.[15] In China, Sun Yat Sen had died and Chiang Kai-Shek had emerged as the new leader of the Chinese Revolution. Mariátegui at first was enthusiastic about Chiang, but the massacre of the Communists in 1928 led him to conclude that the great Chinese Revolution was becoming a tool of bourgeois nationalists. Thermidorian reaction had set in in China also, and Chiang was becoming a fascist dictator of the worst sort.[16] Yet Mariátegui could never become disillusioned with the course of the greatest revolution of all—the Bolshevik Revolution. He discounted the power struggle that had broken out after Lenin's death as a mere transitory event. He wrote that ". . . . the Capitalist world expects a schism in the Russian Revolutionary movement. But that is theoretically and practically impossible due to the internal discipline of the Party."[17]

Yet the great world revolutionary movements' vicissitudes in the late 1920's caused Mariátegui to reconsider the Peruvian situation. Above all he reconsidered his relationship to APRA; he definitely had second thoughts about Haya de la Torre's choice of a revolutionary course. Haya and the APRA were now viewed by Mariátegui as bourgeois and nationalist. He believed that APRA contained all the inherent characteristics that could make it a force of reaction instead of revolution—personalist leadership, lack of ideological commitment to specific goals, and "bourgeois elements" in important leadership positions. Haya de la Torre's apparent quest for personal power seemed to Mariátegui to be incompatible with a sound ideology, and it was ideology above all that spelled the difference between success or failure of a revolution. Haya could well become a reactionary like Chiang. In a letter to Haya de la Torre which precipitated their break, Mariátegui would only support APRA "in principle."[18] Even that support ended as APRA attempted to topple Leguía by violence in the spring of 1927.

The attempted APRA coup did not become public knowledge until Leguía's police began to round up suspects *en masse*. Leguía still viewed *Amauta* as a front for APRA and in the crackdown *Amauta* was closed. Mariátegui and his followers were imprisoned along with all the *apristas* that Leguía's police could locate. The regime justified the mass arrests by stating that it had discovered a Communist conspiracy to seize power by force. Evidence was based on information apparently divulged by British police following a raid on the Soviet Consulate in London. A plot did indeed exist, but its Communist affiliation was open to serious question.

According to the account of Haya de la Torre (and his was the only one available outside of brief news articles), one of his APRA agents, a man named Iparraguirre, went from Mexico to Cuba and then to Peru. There he was to take command of an armed force of some 2500 men staging at Talara where an uprising was to coincide with strikes and demonstrations in other major cities. Mariátegui had been asked to support the venture but had refused, and Leguía got wind of the plan and struck first. Iparraguirre was captured and was forced to "confess" that he had been in the pay of the Soviet Union.

Haya never forgave Mariátegui for not joining him in the uprising. Despite the fact that the success of the operation was dubious from the start, he attributed Mariátegui's reluctance to cowardice and indecision. In a direct reference to Mariátegui, Haya wrote bitterly, "The blood of Iparraguirre has paid for the metaphysical games of the intellectuals."[19]

Mariátegui was held for a time at the military hospital of San Bartolomé. He immediately wrote a letter to the editor of

La Crónica denying his complicity in the APRA plot. He
stated that he was a Marxist, and that his journal *Amauta* did
not call for armed revolt, merely ideological definition. "I am
far from any creole plots," he wrote ". . . The word revolution has another significance, another meaning."[20] Yet Mariátegui never explicitly denied that he was a Communist, nor did
he deny his alleged connections with the Soviet Union. He
merely stated that no document existed that could prove Leguía's allegations. He further argued that no documents were
found at the Soviet Consulate in London that were even
remotely related to Latin America.[21] Mariátegui now was in a
difficult position. Leguía thought he was an Aprista or a
Communist—or both. From the time of his release from prison
he was constantly harassed by the police. In addition, he had
incurred the undying hatred of Haya de la Torre for his refusal
to join in the attempted coup. Seemingly unconcerned, Mariátegui again took up his struggle in December of 1927. The police permitted *Amauta* to reappear thus beginning the second
stage of its existence.

The first issue that was published after the police ban had
been lifted took up the dispute with APRA once more. Mariátegui wrote a vigorous attack on the "creole oppositionist"
tendencies of APRA and the "dictatorial" rule of Haya de la
Torre. Entitled "The Second Act," the substance of Mariátegui's position is reproduced below.

All of the readers of *Amauta* are acquainted with the reasons
why our journal has ceased publication until now. We will not
dwell on the consideration of an incident that . . . has now
been left behind in our journey. A new fact wholly claims us:
the reappearance of *Amauta*. We are interested in the goal
rather than the route. The temporary closing of *Amauta* more
fittingly belongs to its biography than to its life. Intellectual
labor, when it is not metaphysical but dialectical, that is to say
historical, has its risks. For whom is it not evident in the con-

temporary world, that this is a new kind of occupational hazard?

The life of the classic creole "oppositions" was only a series of dramatic protests. Protest first through abuse, followed by disuse, is now discredited in Peru. Mere protest concealed at bottom, a certain intellectual insolvency that necessitated, like the artistic insolvency of a bad stage play, misrepresentation through bravado, intrigue, and theatrical display [*latiguillo*]. Where before one applied oneself to speech, one must now apply oneself to thought. After all it is progress. Speech contented itself with anecdotal usefulness; it requires now a historical quality. We will gain in germinal ideas what we lost in editorial articles and engraved phrases—if in our case this could have been lost. [Mariátegui here referred to the loss of the APRA contributors].

This issue is not a resurrection—*Amauta* could not die. It would always have risen from the dead on the third day. It has never been so alive within, and outside Peru as in those months of silence. We have felt that it was defended by the best Hispanic American spirits.

I have nothing more to say about this reappearance or continuation, but to restate my gratitude to those in Peru and America who have inspired my faith and sustained my hope. The readers know the rest. I repeat, let us wipe out useless words.[22]

Amauta was not now merely concerned with ideological definition, but with the "correctness" of the revolutionaries' ideology. While paying tribute to "the alliance of all free spirits," Mariátegui had become in fact a rigid ideologue who was intolerant of all dissent. It is this position that characterized the second stage of *Amauta*. He could never share leadership, or play a secondary role in any movement. By now he was convinced that he alone possessed the truth, the understanding of history that was the key to Peru's future. Only under his guidance could socialism be successfully achieved. The dispute with APRA over objectives and tactics forced Mariátegui to consider

the very basic matter of *achieving* socialism. He began to
sharpen his ideological position, and to consider revolution in
more than rhetorical phrases as the following passage indicates.

> . . . The other political sector [APRA] is one that I will
> never be able to understand; that of mediocre reformism, of
> domesticated socialism, of pharisean democracy. Furthermore,
> if the revolution necessitates violence, authority and discipline, I
> am for violence, authority, and discipline. I accept these *in toto*
> with all their horrors, without cowardly reservations.[23]

The year 1928 marked a turning point for the now divergent
revolutionary groups in Peru. By now these were several
groups, each claiming to be more revolutionary than the other.
The APRA-Mariátegui dispute no doubt helped the cause of
the Communists in Mariátegui's organization. Mariátegui, an
invalid whose strength was ebbing away each day, was increasingly influenced by his Communist colleagues.

The third stage of *Amauta* (numbers 17–29) began in mid-
1928. Mariátegui's position became even more militant and
extreme. An example of this shift can be seen in the article
below. Entitled "Anniversary and Balance," he reviewed the
two years of *Amauta's* existence, set its future goals, and once
again struck out at APRA.

> *Amauta* is not a diversion, nor merely a game of intellectuals;
> it professes an historic idea, it confesses an active, mass faith, it
> obeys a contemporary social movement. In the struggle between
> two systems, between two ideas—Capitalism and Socialism—it
> does not strike us to consider ourselves as mere spectators, nor
> to invent a third goal. Originality at all costs is a literary and
> anarchical preoccupation. On our banner we inscribe just this
> sole, simple, and great word—Socialism. (With this slogan, we
> affirm our absolute independence in the face of a petty-bour-
> geois and demagogic nationalist party.)[24]

In this essay, Mariátegui also outlined the role of *Amauta* as
a journal of the Socialist Party which he was then organizing.

He stated that the period of ideological definition was over and that it was now time to put that ideology into practical application.

> The work of ideological definition [he wrote] appears to us to be complete. . . . The first stage of *Amauta* has ended. . . . In the second stage, it is not now nec   ̶̶ ̶ ̶ a "journal of the new generation," of the "vangi   In order to be faithful to the Revolution, it is enough that it be called a socialist journal.[25]

In October of 1928, following this call for political action, Mariátegui founded the journal *Labor*. *Labor* was an adjunct of *Amauta*. Its task was to transmit the *doctrinal* basis for revolution in terms that the workers could understand. Just as *Amauta* had the task of mobilizing the intellectuals, *Labor* was to mobilize the workers. Mariátegui evidently believed that the intellectuals had been sufficiently mobilized so that the second stage of the revolutionary struggle could begin. This was to be the mobilization of the proletariat by creating a sense of class consciousness that would draw them into the Socialist Party.[26]

Labor, which contained mostly reprints from *Amauta*, never achieved the stature of the latter journal. Nor did it reflect any new direction in Mariátegui's thought. Ten issues appeared before the journal fell victim to Leguía's police. The core of Mariátegui's thought was expressed in *Amauta*, and in 1928 he selected the best of his *Amauta* articles for publication in book form. The book appeared under the title *Siete ensayos de interpretación de la realidad peruana* (Seven Essays of Interpretation of Peruvian Reality). This was his major work and has gone through ten editions to date. In the 1930's some of his other essays from *Amauta* were collected and published posthumously under the title *Defensa del marxismo* (Defense of Marxism). The essays in these two works form the core of Mariátegui's thought. They also place his political activities in perspective—a perspective that is crucial to understanding

Mariátegui's creation of the "myth" of Peruvian social revolution. The two following chapters analyze these essays in the context of his concept of "Peruvian Reality." It is this concept which attempted to resolve the problem of cultural pluralism by creating an ideological basis for national integration.

7

Los Siete Ensayos

The *Siete ensayos* were an attempt to develop a specific revolutionary program for Peru. Their appearance in 1928 marks the end of relative political detachment and the beginning of Mariátegui's career as a political activist. It is not quite clear whether Mariátegui actually intended to move from his world of speculation and theorizing to the realm of political activism, or whether this was due to the turn of events in Peru. On his return from Europe he believed that his task of ideological definition and preparation for the inevitable revolution would be a lifetime endeavor. Yet, by the seventeenth issue of *Amauta* we know that he believed that this period had been completed. He had revised his estimate of the revolutionary situation by September of 1927. Therefore, the next logical step was to organize the forces to put the revolutionary ideology into practice.

We know that Mariátegui was deeply concerned over the bitter dispute that had destroyed the unity of the revolutionaries in Peru. He was especially sensitive to the charges that he was a *"europeanizante"* who represented an alien philosophy and program. We must remember that the essays that Mariátegui compiled had been originally published during the height of the Mariátegui-Haya de la Torre polemic. It is quite likely then that the *Siete ensayos* also represented an attempt on Mariátegui's part, to state a position that was clearly independent of Haya and the APRA movement. The *Siete ensayos* therefore, can be viewed in the same perspective as *Amauta*

—in the light of the continuing dispute among the left-wing revolutionaries. Before reviewing and analyzing the essays in detail, some preliminary remarks are in order.

The kind of society that Mariátegui envisioned for Peru, which took form in the *Siete ensayos,* was one founded upon the corporate values and institutions of the ancient Incas. This "new" Peru was to be a society that recognized the value of its indigenous heritage. It was supposed to incorporate elements of that heritage into its social structure. Mariátegui attempted to justify the existence of indigenous socialism in a modern society through Marxist arguments.

The Marxist element in Mariátegui's thought was his methodological tool for interpreting the dominant theme in Peruvian political thought—the indigenous theme. While he couched his arguments for indigenous socialism in the language of Marxism, he never adequately established the relationship of indigenous socialism to modern Marxist socialism. It is not suprising that in attempting to relate the two socialisms, the logical rigor of Mariátegui's analysis often broke down.

It is difficult to separate Mariátegui's indigenous ideas from his Marxist analysis. However, this is exactly what has happened to Mariátegui's thought in present-day Peru. His Marxist analysis has been separated from his call for the building of a uniquely Peruvian society. An analysis of the Marxism of Mariátegui will follow in the next chapter. For the present, it is sufficient to sketch his views of Marxism as they related to the *Siete ensayos.*

Mariátegui was captivated by the romantic era of revolutionary Marxism that characterized the decade after the Bolshevik Revolution. Through Marxism he had found a meaning and purpose in life—a dedication to the cause of revolution. This attachment to Marxism was irrational—he accepted the doctrine more on faith than logic, which may account for the breakdown of his Marxist analysis of Peruvian society at very critical junctures in his *Siete ensayos.* Marxism was for Mariátegui the method for interpreting and ordering an otherwise incomprehensible world.

> The Marxist position [he noted] for the non-utopian, contemporary intellectual, is the only position that offers him the road to liberty and advancement. . . . Dogma is not an itinerary, but a compass on the journey. In order to think with freedom, the first condition is to abandon the preoccupation with absolute liberty.[1]

This interpretation of the "spirit" rather than the "letter" of revolutionary Marxism helped establish Mariátegui as an independent Marxist theoretician in Latin America. He attempted to articulate a position that separated him from Haya de la Torre, but in doing so he also incurred the opposition of the Communists, who saw him as a dangerous populist reformer who had corrupted Marxism. This position, first developed in the *Siete ensayos,* led to Mariátegui's ultimate censure in 1929 by the First International Communist Party Congress of Latin America.[2]

The independent position that Mariátegui sought to carve out in the *Siete ensayos* was his attempt to discover and mobilize the revolutionary forces in Peru. The essays were to be a justification for political action, but not the actual program for action. The *Siete ensayos* were to be followed by a treatise on techniques of political action. This treatise was never published; but there is no doubt about the existence of such a manuscript. Mariátegui often mentioned this manuscript in letters and conversations with his associates. He had completed a first draft; and one copy had been sent to a friend in Spain for his comments. Later, in an exchange of letters, this friend denied ever receiving such a manuscript from Mariátegui. Quite likely Mariátegui retained another copy, but all of his papers were confiscated by the police after his death, and they have never been recovered.[3] His plan probably was to define the revolutionary situation as he saw it in Peru, through the

Siete ensayos, and *then* present his program for action—quite
likely in the missing manuscript which was entitled, "Points of
View on the Socialist Revolution in Peru."[4]

The *Siete ensayos* were Mariátegui's effort to appear more
Peruvian and more revolutionary than his rivals. They must be
viewed in the light of the continuing struggle among the revolutionaries in Peru. By 1928, Mariátegui was fully convinced
that the APRA was a mere nationalist movement that was
becoming a fascist organization under the personalist leadership of Haya de la Torre. He believed that APRA would suffer
the same fate as the Kuomintang in China, and that Haya was
an opportunist without an ideology. Mariátegui wanted to
create the ideology of the socialist revolution in Peru: to show
where, why, and how he differed from Haya de la Torre. Only
in this way could Haya be discredited, and shown up as the
charlatan that Mariátegui believed him to be. Through the *Siete
ensayos* Mariátegui attempted to develop an ideology which
would restore unity to the revolutionaries once more. It would
put an end to the meaningless doctrinal debates that had so
splintered the movement.[5]

The first thing that strikes the reader of these essays is Mariátegui's view of history. He saw the history of Peru as a dialectical process that had begun with the Inca Empire. This
process had been interrupted by the Conquest and the subsequent imposition of Spanish rule on the indigenous peoples.
Mariátegui wanted to begin that process anew, to re-cycle the
Peruvian historical process that had been interrupted by the
Conquest. The glories of the great Inca Empire, which were
just being discovered by Peruvians in Mariátegui's time,
seemed to be the logical and fundamental point of departure for
the building of a new social and political order. Mariátegui's
Marxist interpretation of Peruvian history viewed that history
as the transcendental march of man from indigenous communism to modern socialism. This was Peru's dialectical path
which he attempted to present in his essays.

Mariátegui thought that it was axiomatic that indigenous communism and modern socialism were compatible. Each of these social systems meant an end to material want; each also gave the individual a sense of identity, since each person was firmly rooted in the societal structure, and was fully aware of his rights and responsibilities. In an essay not included in this collection, Mariátegui had earlier drawn a sharp distinction between the traditionalist, (i.e. "reactionary") and the revolutionary. He stated that tradition and revolution were not mutually exclusive, since the true revolutionary was not against tradition *per se*. Revolution had acquired a literal meaning for Mariátegui when he wrote, "The true revolutionaries never proceed as if history will begin with them. They know that they represent an historical force. . . . There is no conflict between the revolutionary and tradition, for the revolutionary is in tune with history."[6]

For years Peruvians had thought of their heritage as that of the Spanish post-Conquest era. This was an error; Peru's heritage, Mariátegui maintained, was the socialist Inca society, not the feudalistic legacy of Spain. Traditionalism was a complete opposition to change, and this was synonymous with Hispanic feudalism. True revolution, Mariátegui wrote, ". . . is contained in tradition. Outside of tradition, there is nothing but utopia."[7] Revolution in Peru therefore, must be founded upon the tradition that was native to the land. It was this tradition that would integrate and unite the "new" Peruvian nation.

The *Siete ensayos* were clearly not an objective study of Peruvian history. Mariátegui thought he had discovered the dialect of Peruvian history—what the nation was, is, and *ought* to be. Only he and a small group of his followers possessed this "truth" which actually distorted historical facts. He himself admitted this distortion in the preface to his essays:

There is no lack of those who think of me as being Europeanized, alien to the facts and questions of my country. I will allow

my work to vindicate me of this cheap and selfish conjecture. I
have served my best apprenticeship in Europe. And I believe
that the salvation of Indo-America does not exist outside European, or Western science and thought . . .

I repeat again that I am not an impartial and objective critic.
My judgments are nourished by my ideals, by my sentiments,
my passions. I have an avowed and energetic ambition: that of
contributing to the creation of Peruvian socialism.[8]

Throughout the essays Mariátegui attempted to follow the
Marxist analytical approach. Nowhere is this more apparent
than in his view of the economic structure as the crucial determinant of the social and political structure. Change the economic structure and all other changes would follow. This idea
was perhaps Mariátegui's fullest appreciation of the doctrine of
Marx. Actually, his knowledge of Marx stemmed from the
impressions that he had acquired in Europe, especially through
the writings of Barbusse, Croce, and Miguel de Unamuno—the
sources of Marx that he himself cited most frequently. His
knowledge of the Indian was likewise quite limited; and his
comments on the indigenous peoples were more than likely
based on the revived accounts of the Conquest chroniclers and
writers—Las Casas, Acosta, and Garcilaso. With this scanty
background, Mariátegui had set out to re-write Peruvian history as the basis for his ideology of revolutionary change.[9]

Following a preface which denied any pretense of historical
objectivity, Mariátegui began to trace the economic evolution of
Peru.[10] Prior to the Spanish Conquest, an indigenous economy
based on the people and the soil of Peru was developing *spontaneously.* This economic structure had fostered the growth of a
society in which men experienced little material want. Based
on a form of collective farm operation, the economy (and the
state) were also supported by the religious beliefs of the people.
The religion of the people stressed absolute obedience to the
ruler above all else. Because the concept of social duty

(obedience) was developed to such an extraordinary degree, the individualist tendencies of men were greatly subdued.

The Spanish conquerors changed this idyllic state of primitive socialism when they destroyed the Inca state. But the Spaniards were unable to replace the indigenous economic and social system with a "higher" system, i.e., a more efficient one. Upon these ruins of the Inca state, the Spanish imposed a feudal economic system (a step backward in Mariátegui's view) and an alien, other-worldly religion. None of these foreign institutions took root among the indigenous peoples—the remnants of the old culture still dominated the lives of the highland peoples. Only the Jesuits with their "organic positivism" managed to create a social and economic structure that was consistent with the old corporate institutions of the Incas.

The Conquest was presented as a military and ecclesiastical adventure that was rooted in greed. It was *not* a political and economic enterprise in any sense of the word. Spanish greed which, in search of minerals, led to the penetration of the Andean realm of the Indian became the fundamental philosophy of Spanish colonial rule. This philosophy along with the feudal economic structure still endured, even though a bourgeois economy had grown up in the coastal cities. The feudal *hacienda* of the highlands, the "colonialism" of the extractive industries, and the nascent bourgeois-capitalist enclaves in the cities all existed side by side in the Peru of Mariátegui. Moreover, each of these systems existed at the expense of the Indian masses.

The discovery of the guano and nitrate deposits in the first decades of the nineteenth century ended Mariategui's first, or feudal stage of Peruvian history. Coinciding with the independence movement, the guano and nitrate booms ushered in the second stage of Peru's post-Conquest economic history—the colonial epoch, i.e., economic colonialism. Mariátegui interpreted the success of the Latin American independence movements in the light of world economic conditions. In other words, the independence movements corresponded to the dialectical process of world history.

Spain, a feudal state, was bound to lose in her attempt to retain her New World possessions. For feudalism was destined to be replaced by capitalism. Spanish dominance (feudal) in Latin America *had* to be supplanted by British dominance (capitalist). Feudalism had fulfilled its historic mission. It was *inevitably* doomed by the march of capitalism as represented by Great Britain and later the United States. The lesson that Mariátegui drew from this interpretation was that a revolutionary movement, in order to be successful, must be in tune with the (economic) forces of history. Latin American independence had been determined by the historic necessity to develop capitalism. Therefore, the success of the socialists would be determined by the historic need to develop socialism.[11]

Capitalism was aided in its development in Peru by the growth of the guano and nitrate industries, and by the cotton and sugar plantations of the coastal areas. Investment in these enterprises had been encouraged by the military caudillos that ruled Peru during this era. This investment, dominated by British capital, was the key to the growth of the bourgeois enclaves in the cities. Feudalism, however, still held firm in the highlands. Indeed, this feudalism was perpetuated in the nineteenth century even though capitalism was developing in Peru. The descendants of the conquerors, the landed aristocracy, invested in the new industries. Offshoots of the old feudal families had become the new bourgeoisie.

Mariátegui held that the bourgeoisie was obliged by its *historic function* to adopt all of the rhetoric of nineteenth century liberalism. But because of the fusion of the bourgeoisie and the aristocracy in Peru, any thought and action that was related to social change was less defined and more backward than in the United States or Western Europe.[12] The ideas of the French and American Revolutions simply could not take root in such an environment. Throughout the nineteenth century the status quo was maintained in Peru by the bourgeois-aristocratic alliance. Finally, after the debacle of the War of the Pacific, the alliance was institutionalized in the civilista party. Despite these occurrences, Mariátegui still thought that the nineteenth century was an advance over the preceding period of feudal Spanish rule. For with the independence movement and the growth of the new industries, the first leap in the process from feudalism to capitalism had taken place.[13]

Continuing his economic analysis of Peruvian history, Mariátegui wrote that the final stage of Peru's evolution toward socialism had begun in the post-war period. Like many Peruvian writers, he viewed the post-war period as that period following the Second War of the Pacific. Because of this great national disaster the forces of production completely collapsed. The guano and nitrate revenues dried up, and the economy was completely wrecked by military mis-rule. Since that time (from roughly 1885 on) foreign investors had gained control of most of the nation's industries and its communications network. Mariátegui still believed that Peru lived in this epoch. Since this period immediately pre-dated the revolutionary era that Mariátegui foresaw, it is well to note his outline of this stage of history.

1. The appearance of a modern industrial sector.

2. An increased role of finance capital, especially foreign banks operating in Peru.

3. Shortening of the distances between Peru, the United States, and Western Europe, following the opening of the Panama Canal.

4. A gradual shift from British economic hegemony to United States dominance of the Peruvian economy.

5. The development of a capitalist class. Agrarian property retained its social and political influence, but the value of the old viceregal titles had declined.

6. The modern *El Dorado* myth of great treasure that lay in the rubber industry of the Amazon was completely shattered.

7. A rise in the prices of the commodities that Peru sold on the world market, causing a rapid growth of private fortunes. The coast exercised an increasing dominance in the life of the nation.

8. The reestablishment of Peruvian international credit, and the shift of the national debt from London to New York banks where better terms were available.[14]

At this juncture in his analysis, Mariátegui attempted to explain why Peru was a society in which classic Marxist principles could not be applied. Marxism he stated, must be adapted to the existing conditions in Peru. Unlike Western Europe, *three* economies existed at the same historical period: feudal *haciendas*, a bourgeois economy, and indigenous communism. The first two of these economies were built on the semi-feudal base of exploitation of the Indian masses. The root of Peru's social and economic problems lay in the tenacious survival of feudalism.

In Mariátegui's view Peru was still an agrarian society. However, agricultural production was inefficient. Where it was advanced (on the coastal plantations), its production was geared to the demands of the world market. This created a situation that forced Peru to import substantial quantities of foodstuffs just to feed the populace. The best lands were being used to satisfy the demands of foreign markets. Furthermore,

Mariátegui held that urban life was languid and poor. The small town was practically non-existent because of the dominance of the rural hacienda system. Peru was wholly unlike Europe where the village proceeded from the gradual collapse of feudalism, thereby fostering the growth of capitalism. The self-contained life of the highland haciendas and the coastal estates had "impeded" the development of a "true" form of capitalism in Peru.[15]

Because of the development of Peru's economy, Mariátegui believed that only a destruction of the feudal economic and social system would advance the cause of socialism. Once this destruction had been accomplished, Mariategui proposed to establish a capitalist system! Capitalism in his view was both an economic system and a psychological disposition which made men receptive to social change. "Capitalism," he wrote, "is an urban phenomenon. It has the spirit of the industrial, manufacturing, and mercantile town. For this reason one of the first acts of capitalism was the liberation of the land, the destruction of feudalism. The development of the city necessitates its nourishing itself on the free activity of the peasant."[16]

Since the fostering of the growth of capitalism hinged on land-reform and the freeing of the peasant from feudal bondage, Mariátegui proceeded to outline his solution for the Indian and land problems. His essay, which was an expansion of an article originally written for the Soviet news journal *Tass*, stated that the solution to the Indian problem was to be found in the economic structure of Peru, not in vague educational or social welfare programs.[17] In developing this line of reasoning, Mariátegui obviously twisted historical fact to suit his argument. He held that the Conquest was a tremendous carnage, estimating that the indigenous population was *no less* than ten million at the time of the arrival of the Spaniards in Peru. In three centuries of alien rule, he estimated some *nine million* Indians had perished. (In the 1920's the Indian population was around four million, in 1962, slightly under six million.) Mariategui also included the entire Inca Empire in his estimate, fully a third of which was outside the present boundaries of Peru. But even at that his estimate is at least four million too high. Quite likely he drew his figures from the early post-Conquest accounts of pro-Indian clerics. Whether realizing it or not, he had once again raised the spectre of the old Black Legend to justify his condemnation of the existing order.[18]

The peasant masses that Mariátegui believed he had "discovered" constituted the bulk of his Peruvian proletariat. It was this great mass of people that once mobilized would be the arm of a socialist revolution. However, instead of going to these Indian masses directly, Mariátegui followed the approach advocated by González Prada. He wanted to first mobilize the radical intellectuals and urban workers before carrying the struggle to the highlands. Yet his appeals were not to be self-interest of these urban groups. Rather, Mariátegui attempted to awaken their idealism and their nationalist sentiments. They were the vanguard of a movement that would destroy the old, and build a new Peru. This vanguard in his view, should place the goal of the revolution ahead of any sordid self-interest. This revolution's primary aim was the "redemption" of the indigenous peoples. It was to be a crusade to return Peru to the "true" Peruvians—the Indians and *mestizos*.

According to Mariátegui, the feudalism which held the Indian in bondage should have been liquidated in the nineteenth century when bourgeois capitalism was emerging. This did not occur, nor was the Indian "redeemed" by the humanistic, moral movements of the late nineteenth, and early twentieth centuries. Mariátegui believed that the Indian himself had to be aroused by the revolutionary example of the intellectuals and the urban proletariat. Only the Indian could succeed in the realization of his rightful claim to the land; only he could end his own abject servitude. "A people of four million men," wrote Mariátegui, "conscious of their numbers, will never despair for their future. The same four million men, as long as they are an organic mass, a dispersed multitude, are incapable of determining their historic path."[19]

A successful revolution would occur through the action of a mass organization conscious of its historic mission, guided by an elite which was determined to achieve its destiny at any cost. The threat of violence was implicit in this theory. The entrenched ruling classes were not likely to surrender their economic and political hegemony without a struggle. The *Siete ensayos* intended to prepare the revolutionary forces for that inevitable struggle which was world-wide in scope. "It is the myth, it is the idea of socialist revolution. . . . The same myth, the same idea are the decisive agents in the awakening other old races in collapse, Hindus, Chinese, etc."[20] Mariátegui intended to be the Lenin of Peru's indigenous proletariat.

We have seen that Mariátegui viewed the land and Indian questions as interrelated factors. They were the keys to his analysis of "Peruvian reality," though that analysis was not as scientifically dispassionate as he had claimed. If anything, his essays were a continuation of the romantic arguments of nineteenth-century *gonzálezpradismo*. The main difference was that the indigenous themes were now presented as "scientific" truths.[21] They were presented in a more modern form of discourse—the language of Marxism. Yet Mariátegui himself could not totally divest himself of the romantic elements of the Peruvian *indigenista* tradition. In one of his essays he remarked in a very un-Marxian aside that those who studied the Indian and agrarian problems from a socialist point of view, were really continuing the "apostolic" battle of the great colonial defender of the Indian, Father Bartolomé de Las Casas.[22]

The great problems of land-reform, and the incorporation of the Indian into the social fabric of the nation was not even close to a solution in the 1920's. To a socialist critic like Mariátegui the reasons were patently obvious. Primarily, the ruling classes paid lip-service to the Indians' just claims on the land. But while they justified those claims on moral grounds, they failed to comprehend the *material* grounds for those claims (i.e., that those claims were consistent with the inexorable march of history).[23] In addition, the ruling classes tended to treat agrarian problems as technical ones, capable of solution through the application of new scientific techniques. Mere tinkering with a feudal system by technicians and agronomists would not solve the problem. What was really necessary, Mariátegui argued, was a complete change of the economic and social system.

In calling for this sweeping change, he showed no concern for the technical problems inherent in such a massive reform program. Clearly, Mariátegui had no idea himself how to make Peru agriculturally self-sufficient.[24] He abruptly ended his sweeping condemnation of the Spanish colonial and the republican eras with the remark that his analysis had proceeded from the point of view of, "practical, concrete, and material usefulness."[25] He did not place the Indian and land problems in a new perspective; he merely called for a sweeping change, yet never outlined how this change was to be accomplished.

Having described the first cause of Peruvian ills—the economic system—Mariátegui then proceeded with an analysis of the political system. In colonial times the basic communal unit, the *ayllu* (which he compared to the *mir* of pre-revolutionary Russia) was recognized and protected by Spanish law. But this law had never actually been observed in Peru. Despite the destruction of the communal agricultural system, which was the economic base of the *ayllu,* the *social* institution of the *ayllu* still survived in the highland communities. Indigenous socialism had endured the imposition of an alien feudalism.[26]

The republican state which emerged after the wars of independence did not develop from a conflict between the landholding aristocracy and the bourgeois merchant as had been the case in modern Europe. Rather, in the Peruvian case, these theoretically antagonistic classes had collaborated throughout the nineteenth century. Therefore, the liberal-based laws of the nineteenth-century republic were rooted in the same feudal absolutism of the Spanish colonial period. They were powerless to foster the growth of capitalism in the European sense. Independence and the establishment of a republic had not advanced Peru to the next stage (capitalism) of the historical process. Since capitalism had not been established, the wars of independence had not been revolutions at all. They had been merely revolts to break away from Spanish imperial rule.[27]

In following this line of reasoning, Mariátegui began to consider in a peripheral way, what he meant by revolution. Basically, it was the process by which an organic, corporatistic society would be realized. This society was represented by the indigenous structure of pre-Conquest Peru, and by the modern social and economic system of socialism. *His* revolution was an attempt to achieve such a society in Peru—modern socialism combined with the indigenous institutions that were compatible with that system. It was in this way that man's march through history became understandable to Mariátegui. Socialism did not reject historical experience; it was the culmination of that experience.

It was this unusual concept of revolution that led Mariátegui to conclude that the only way that feudalism could be eliminated in Peru was to foster the creation of a bourgeois-capitalist class. He made this position not in his *Siete ensayos* (where one might expect to find such relevant ideas) but buried in an introduction to Luis Valcárcel's book, *Tempest in the Andes:*

> Revolutionary, and even reformist thought cannot now be liberal but socialist. Socialism appears in our history not by reason of chance, of imitation, or of being in vogue as superficial spirits suppose, but as an historic fatality. And it happens that while on the one hand those of us who profess socialism propose logically and coherently, the reorganization of the country upon socialist bases—we maintain that the economic and political regime which we are battling has gradually turned into a force for the colonization of the country by foreign capitalist imperialists—we proclaim that the latter is an instance in

our history when it is not possible to be truly nationalist and revolutionary without being socialist; on the other hand there does not exist in Peru, as there has never existed, a progressive minded bourgeoisie with a nationalist feeling that professes itself to be liberal and democratic, whose policy is inspired by the postulates of its doctrine . . .

Few critical and profound minds can suppose that the liquidation of feudalism is the task of the typically liberal and bourgeois, and that to attempt to convert it to a socialist function is to romantically twist the laws of history. This simplistic criterion of the theoreticians of little depth opposes socialism with little more argument that capitalism has not fulfilled its mission in Peru. The surprise of capitalism's advocates will be extraordinary when they learn that the function of socialism in the governing of the nation according to its historical course and direction, will be in large measures that of realizing capitalism—that is to say the still historically vital possibilities of capitalism—in the sense that it is suitable to the interests of social progress.[28]

Throughout his essays Mariátegui's main indictment of those who had shaped Peru's history was that they never knew history's laws. Therefore, these classes (and individuals) had not fulfilled their "historic functions." It was the task of the socialist revolutionaries, who knew the laws of history and their own "function," to get Peru moving once again on the road to socialism. The claim that only the socialists knew the course of history, and could achieve history's destiny, was the claim that legitimized any attempt to overthrow the existing order.

In the nineteenth century the military rulers had been mere interpreters of the wishes of the landed aristocracy—their "fiduciaries." In the twentieth century the landed aristocracy was still a potent power in Peru. Together with foreign interests, these dominant classes stifled the growth of a vigorous bourgeoisie.[29] The forces which controlled Peru's destiny were reactionary. Therefore it was quite legitimate to remove them by any and all possible means.

The application of the liberal concept of private property was an example of how the economic growth of Peru was retarded by the ruling elite. In the hands of the forces of "reaction," the concept of private property served an anti-social function in Peru. Instead of moving the Indian from a position of servitude to that of a free salaried worker (a "progressive" step on the way to socialism) the idea of private property had fostered the continued existence of the feudal latifundia system. The concept of private property had never extended to the Indian. Latifundia continued to erode the economic and juridical institutions of the ancient indigenous civilization.[30]

In considering the idea of private property, Mariátegui also commented on the relationship of individual liberty to socialism. Individual liberty, he thought, was the root cause of the evil that had befallen mankind in modern times. The quest for individual liberty had set man against man in a senseless quest for material gain. Man was forced to live contrary to his very nature. Socialism on the other hand would end this unnatural state of affairs.

In a socialist society, men lived once more in the shelter of the collective, or corporate way of life. All men would be mutually dependent on one another, and none would seek advantage over the others. This conception of the good society (the socialist society), was as deeply rooted in the tradition of Spanish mediaeval and Mediterranean thought, as it was in Marx. (For Mariátegui, the Hispanic mediaeval influences may have been more influential, considering the impact that the Spanish mystics and Unamuno had upon him.) Mariátegui's arguments for the creation of a socialist state were same arguments that had been used to justify Syndicalism in the Mediterranean countries. Like Ortega y Gasset and Benedetto Croce, Mariátegui attacked the capitalist creation of the mass-man. He would have the individual firmly rooted in an institutional place where both the individual and society would be secure.

The Mediterranean influence on Mariátegui's line of reasoning can best be seen in his attempt to distinguish modern communism from indigenous Inca communism. Here he treated the corporate society of the Incas in much the same fashion as Spanish and Italian writers had depicted mediaeval society—an almost ideal state of nature, violated by the capitalist forces that destroyed it. (Only in Mariátegui's account, the forces of feudalism, not capitalism, had violated the ideal state of the Incas.)

> Modern communism [he wrote] is distinct from indigenous communism. This is the first thing that one must learn and understand when exploring *Twantinsuyo*. One and another communism are products of different human experiences. They belong to distinct historical epochs. They constitute an elaboration of dissimilar civiliations. That of the Incas was an agrarian civilization. That of Marx and Sorel was an industrial civilization. In the former Man yields to Nature. In the latter Nature yields at times to Man. . . . The man of *Twantinsuyo* never felt any necessity for individual liberty. . . . The Inca regime was certainly theocratic and despotic, but this is a trait of all the regimes of antiquity. . . . The *ayllu*—the community—was the cell of the empire. The Incas made unity; they invented the empire, but they did not create the cell. The juridical state organized by the Incas, reproduced without a doubt *the pre-existing natural state* [italics added]. The Incas violated nothing. . . . In the Inca society robbery did not exist. Or if you wish, a socialist organization existed.[31]

This state of nature "that violated nothing" could not be obliterated by the Conquest; for Mariátegui noted that these noble indigenous peoples still retained their "superior" habits of cooperation and group solidarity despite centuries of exploitation. The ideas of liberalism (especially that of private property), never touched the Indian. Mariátegui noted with an air of triumph that, "the Indian, despite a hundred years of legislation of the republican regime, still has not been made an individualist."[32]

Mariátegui's plan for the establishment of socialism in Peru, called for a return to a society that was closest to "the preexisting natural state." The main obstacle to such a return was the latifundia system, which attacked not only the economic base of Indian society, but also sought not the destruction of the *ayllu,* ". . . the social institution that defends indigenous tradition, and that preserves the function of the peasant family."[33] The existing order was therefore illegitimate, since it was "unnatural." The sole basis for the legitimacy of the Peruvian state, in Mariátegui's view, was the degree that it conformed to the indigenous institutions of its people.

The creation of the kind of society that Mariátegui envisioned was also hampered by Peru's economic ties to an alien market centered in New York and London. The development of a Peruvian economy was retarded by this economic state of affairs. Valuable foreign exchange earned through the sale of primary products, was spent on the importation of foodstuffs and luxury items rather than on the development of the economy. As long as this practice continued Peru would always be, ". . . a deposit of raw materials, and a store for the sale of foreign manufacturers."[34]

Mariátegui abruptly ended this analysis of economic growth with a series of "final propositions." He stated that there was a "fundamental and organic difference between a feudal, semifeudal, and capitalist economy." (Though that difference was never explained.) He closed with an attack on the latifundia system that bore little relationship to the theme of indigenous socialism that he had laboriously developed. Almost half of the total length of the *Siete ensayos* is devoted to the development of the theme of indigenous socialism and its relationship to modern socialism. Yet Mariátegui completely ignored this relationship in his concluding remarks. The evil latifundia system became *not* a barrier to the advancement and integration of the Indian, but a barrier to the immigration of white European peasant farmers.[35]

The logic of his arguments in the *Siete ensayos* became more confusing as Mariátegui moved on to an analysis of the Peruvian educational system and the Latin American University Reform Movement. He praised the Reform Movement of 1919 as, ". . . the birth of a new Latin American generation . . ." a generation that was the most deeply affected by ". . . the messianic sentiments, the revolutionary aspirations, and the mystic passion peculiar to the post-war period."[36] This period had begun when the American president, Woodrow Wilson, made the cause of the war against the Central Powers an ideological one. That cause was "a war to end all wars," and a battle for "the right of self-determination of all peoples." In the immediate postwar period this "myth," this ideology was beginning to backfire on the capitalist West as the Bolshevik Revolution and the revolutionary surge among the colonial peoples had shown.

Mariátegui theorized that unrest among the university students was caused by the economic condition of the post-war world. The middle classes that had grown so rapidly before and during the Great War, were now caught in an economic squeeze following the end of hostilities. This phenomenon had "proletarianized" the middle class (Mariátegui did not regard the middle-class as a class at all, merely a "zone of transition" between the aristocracy and the proletariat).[37] It was this process of middle-class "proletarianization" that led to the University Reform Movement. In this dialectical approach, the "proletarianization" of classes began when capitalism had reached the ". . . determined conditions of its economic development."[38] Yet Mariátegui had earlier gone to great lengths to tell us that capitalism had *not* developed in Peru, and that the socialists themselves would have to create it. Now Mariátegui tells us that capitalism had reached its apogee in Peru (and in the rest of Latin America), and that this had caused the University Reform Movement.

Obviously Mariátegui had fallen into a logical morass. He had previously attacked the universities as bastions of aristocratic rule that educated only the wealthy. Now we are led to believe that the students are middle class and have become "proletarianized." (Proletarianization meant that the students had become conscious of their identity as a class, and of their revolutionary role in making a socialist revolution.) Yet Mariátegui still argued that the universities were bastions of upper class rule and called for the incorporation of "extra university values" into university life. This meant a politicization of the university environment so as to destroy this "bastion of feudalism," and make the universities political agents of economic and social reform.[39]

Mariátegui stated that the University Reform Movement in Latin America and the socialist gains in the world had been nullified in the post-war era by renascent capitalism, and the "reactionary" offensive of fascism.[40] Yet the process of "proletarianization" had continued. He linked this process to the theme of man's increasing alienation in a modernizing society. Without having read Marx's early writings, he stated the central position of Marx—mankind had been enslaved by an industrial machine. This machine had deformed the very essence and ends of work and art. The secular, individualistic society of capitalism had to be changed or destroyed if this dehumanizing process was to end. Then, without so much as a pause, Mariátegui completely dropped this potentially explosive theme and returned once more to the concept of indigenous socialism. He condemned the Peruvian educational system for not helping the Indian to better his lot. Then he contradicted his own argument by returning to González Prada's position that, "To teach him to read and write is not to educate him."[41]

This cursory analysis of the University Reform Movement

and the Peruvian educational system ended abruptly with an
impassioned appeal for unspecified reforms based on the usual
"concrete social and economic reasons." These same "reasons"
were appealed to in an essay dealing with religion in Peru.
Like many Latin Americans who have written about the religious aspect of their culture, Mariátegui compared the Conquest and the imposition of Catholicism on Latin America with
the Puritan and Protestant influences on North America. After
some meandering through New England and Mexico, he
finally arrived at the heart of his essay—the relationship of
religion to the state.[42]

In Mariátegui's view the Inca religion, like Marxism, was
fundamentally a materialist and collectivist belief system. It
was a moral and juridical code, rather than a metaphysical
concept. State and Church were one; a fact that made Peru
closer to China and India than to the Christian West. Given
this politico-religious structure in Peru, the Inca religion could
not survive the destruction of the Inca state. Yet this pantheistic
"sentiment" of the Incas was more than just a state religion: its
purpose was the political unification of the empire. Free from
complicated abstractions, its simple allegories were drawn from
the instincts and customs of a nation of agrarian tribes. These
tribes, according to Mariátegui's mis-reading of history, were
more inclined to cooperation than war. (Yet in fact, the Inca
empire was founded upon conquest and war. At the time of the
arrival of the Spaniards the Inca state was crumbling due to
dynastic disputes and territorial over-extension.) Above all else,
in Mariátegui's idealization, all institutions, political and religious, coincided with the economic structure, and the "spirit"
of a sedentary people. The indigenous religion was practical,
resting on "the ordinary and the empirical," not on the won-
der-working virtue of a prophet and his word.

-The Conquest had interrupted this "organic" utopia, and
Catholicism legitimized the imposition of Spanish rule. The
religion of the conquerors however, was unable to extend its

roots deep into the Indian culture despite its ability to absorb many aspects of the traditional belief system. The indigenous cults were still able to survive, since they were part of tradition, and more easily understood than the mysteries of Catholicism. Catholicism's greatest role was in reinforcing the feudal economic system—as long as it remained the dominant religion, capitalism would never take hold in Peru. This argument was buttressed with a quote from Marx: "The money system is essentially Catholic, but the credit system essentially Protestant."[43]

Mariátegui held that there was no atmosphere in Latin America that was really suitable for the ascetic aspects of Catholicism. "Instead of mortification . . . are found greed, lassitude, and a fondness for luxury."[44] Even the nineteenth-century doctrine of classical liberalism was weak and without depth in Latin America. Therefore liberalism could not offer a viable alternative to the doctrine of the established religion. Only in the modern world could one find an effective alternative belief system, a secular doctrine of moral rearmament. The new revolutionary and social "myths" could not occupy the same profound position in the consciences of men as did the old religious myths.[45] Marxism, Mariátegui reasoned, because it was so much like the ancient code of the Inca, would become the new political religion—the juridical and moral foundation of his "new Peru."

Passing from the relationship of religion (or "myth") to the state, Mariátegui proceeded to consider the actual structure of the Peruvian state. The old nineteenth-century federalist-centralist disputes were totally useless in his view since they were merely concerned with administrative reform. Mariátegui cogently argued that the administrative organization of Peru still rested on these arbitrary divisions dating back to the Conquest. Since none of these took into account the needs or wishes of the indigenous peoples, none were, therefore, legitimate. He maintained that the structure and public policies of the state completely ignored the Indian since the state was founded upon exploitation of the Indian.

The only thing that was truly well defined in Peru according to Mariátegui was its geography. The geographical division of the country (coast, mountains, and jungle) was also social and economic as well as geographic. He maintained that Peru should be governed along the lines of these "natural" divisions. The key to this "organic" division of government lay in the development of a trans-Andean communications network. This network would assure that no one city would dominate the life of the country as Lima had done since the Conquest. Mariátegui described the lack of municipal autonomy, pointing to this fact as proof of his charge that Peru was governed much as it had been in colonial times. All administrative positions in the local communities were filled by direct appointment from the center—Lima.

It was obvious that Mariátegui had little concern for the difficult problems inherent in the social and economic changes that he called for. His only formula for governing Peru was presented in the following statement. Peru was to be governed by an, ". . . integrally revised and transformed political and social organization that coincided above all with the economic system."[46]

We now come upon an element in Mariátegui's concept of indigenous socialism which perhaps was suspected earlier. That element is racism. In an essay on Peruvian literature, Mariátegui coupled his idealization of the Inca in literature with a bitter attack on the Negroes of Peru, who comprised less than one per cent of the total population. Mariátegui wrote that, ". . . they look on the sierra with distrust and hostility, and have not been able to acclimate themselves to Peru either physically or spiritually. When the Negro has mixed with the Indian it has been to debase him, communicating to him his flattering domesticity and his exteriorized, morbid psychology."[47]

The closing passages of the *Siete ensayos* contained an eloquent plea for Peruvians to create a new nation founded on the racial and cultural heritage of the Indian. Here Mariátegui echoed the sentiments of the Latin American mestizo who is the product of two worlds—the Iberian and the Indian. Mariátegui's essays are an effort to orient the mestizo (whom he represents) toward the Indian, rather than the Iberian heritage. "The problem of our time," he wrote, "is not knowing what Peru has been . . . but what Peru is. The past interests us as a means of explaining the present. The only thing that survives of Twantinsuyo is the Indian. The biological material of Twantinsuyo is indestructible."[48]

For all their pretensions of scientific analysis, the *Siete ensayos* read like the writings of a dispossessed, rootless man attempting to create the feeling of racial, spiritual, and cultural identity for other dispossessed and rootless men. The arguments of Mariátegui appealed to the like-minded—to those who felt that their lives had somehow been distorted by a social system rooted in concepts of race, class, status, wealth, and family station. There seemed to be little opportunity for men like Mariátegui, who lived in a society that was dominated by a white aristocratic class that refused to admit others into the circle of wealth and power. Mariátegui "The Spokesman" of the "new men of Peru," wanted to bring down that society. He used appeals that were strident, racist, and more nationalist than Marxist. Presented in what was fast becoming the common parlance of his generation, the "new language" of Marxism, his arguments only *appeared* to have the force of logic. We now turn to Mariátegui's Marxism, and its relationship to the indigenous socialism of national integration.

8

The Language and
Symbols of Marxism

In 1927 and 1928, Mariátegui wrote a series of essays for *Amauta* which were entitled, "Defensa del Marxismo" (A Defense of Marxism). These essays were an attempt to prove that Marxism was the *true* revolutionary doctrine for Peru and other "oppressed" countries. The essays also attempted to *disprove* the charges that Marxism was dying as a revolutionary doctrine—an allegation made by some post-war European critics.

Mariátegui did not doubt that the revolutionary élan of Marxism had waned during the two decades between the founding of the Second International and the end of World War I. But he viewed this as merely a time of testing rather than decay. The Bolshevik Revolution and the emergence of a new generation of Marxist thinkers had given renewed vigor to Marxist thought. A true "revision" had come about through the efforts of a new revolutionary generation—Lenin, Mao Tse-Tung, and above all Georges Sorel. These figures, Mariátegui maintained, were the true revisionists, not Eduard Bernstein. Bernstein was a mere "reformist," not a revolutionary.[1]

This resurgence of Marxism after World War I was a major theme of Mariátegui's essays. He attempted to describe this phenomenon, and to interpret its relationship to the predicted socialist revolution in Peru. In these essays, one can clearly see that Mariátegui's application of Marxism to the Peruvian context was actually the creation of a form of national communism—a type of thought not uncommon in today's developing nations. Nationalism was by far the most dominant element in his thought. Later this fact would not pass unnoticed by the Comintern.

Mariátegui's essays on Marxism, combined with the *Siete ensayos* firmly established his reputation as a major revolutionary theoretician in Latin America. Henrí Barbusse, who had taken his *Clarté* group into the French Communist Party, called him the new light of Latin America. Indeed prior to his censure by the Comintern in 1929, Mariátegui was regarded by Moscow as the only Marxist theoretician of any stature in Latin America. His combining of Marxism and nationalism into *one* revolutionary doctrine coincided exactly with the Leninist program of regarding nationalism as an ally of socialism in the revolutionary cause.

It is not necessary to explain the Leninist strategy for world revolution and its subsequent revision by Stalin. It is sufficient to note that 1927 and 1928 were the years in which Mariátegui's influence was at its zenith in Peru and Latin America. This was in part due to the congruence of his ideas and those of the communists. One might conclude that he was a Marxist, and some would say a communist by historical circumstances. That is, Mariátegui's ideology of indigenous socialism, and his interpretations of Marxism exactly fitted the "official" Comintern interpretation. As we shall see, this congruence of Mariátegui's ideas and the "official" ideology of the Comintern ceased in 1929.

Many students and intellectuals in Peru were attracted to Mariátegui because they too opposed the personalist leadership of Haya de la Torre. Some of these who later became active in the Communist Party, believed that Mariátegui was developing a truly Peruvian, and Latin American line of Marxist thought. They soon discovered that this was not the case. Rather, Mariátegui's interpretation of Marxism was a *personal,* not a national or universal one—his Marxist ideology was based on idealism, not realism. Moreover, while he professed his materialism he was more concerned with the *spiritual* promise of Marxism. For Mariátegui, Marxism was more symbolic than substantive. It was his personal *weltanschauung*, a credo that ordered the world and gave personal meaning to his troubled existence. This personal ethic was shot through with logical inconsistencies. Yet when projected to the level of a political doctrine, it seemed to possess many aspects of a modern nation- alist ideology.

Through the years Mariátegui's appeals to Peruvian nation- alism have survived in the rhetoric of Peru's reform-oriented ideologies. Yet the Marxist content of those appeals has faded into obscurity. The probable reason is that nationalism, unlike his Marxism, has had greater appeal in Peru. His nationalism was only loosely tied to his personal, religious-like belief in Marxism. In essence, Mariátegui propounded two political philosophies—one Marxist and one nationalist. The *public* political philosophy was the revolutionary nationalism inherent in his concept of *indigenismo* and the founding of a "new" Peru. His private or personal political philosophy was that of Marxism. Mariátegui's Marxism contained the spiritual prom- ise of personal redemption through revolutionary activity. This was difficult to transmit to others. This personal endless "agonic" struggle never became the institutional and organiza- tional base for his ideology of indigenous Peruvian socialism. His public political philosophy—indigenous socialism—has survived, but his personal philosophy, Marxism, has become a very minor part of the Mariátegui legend and legacy in Peru. *Defensa del Marxismo* explains in large part why this is so.

In his first essay, Mariátegui stated that the revitalization and continuation of the great work of Marx, had been most successfully carried out by Georges Sorel. It was Sorel who had re-created the revolutionary élan of the early Marxism. This élan had been lacking in the late nineteenth century due to the "bourgeois intellectualism and parliamentarianism" that had corrupted the movement.[2] Sorel's theory of revolutionary myths

once again gave a form of religious expression and experience
to the philosophy of Marx. The "new" Marxism of Sorel had
clarified the role of violence (the general strike), as the instrument of bringing about revolution.

In this opening essay, Mariátegui became ensnared in
semantic difficulties. He never defined his terms and often sub-
stituted one term for another without explanation. A most
obvious example is the way in which he used the terms revolution (*revolución*) and renovation (*renovación*). Indeed, his
interpretation of the revitalization of Marxism is in the spirit of
renovation, a return to original Marxist concepts, especially
primitive communism. *Renovación* is most adequately translated as renewal. But this is also the meaning that the term
revolución conveys in Mariátegui's writings. Mariátegui used
these terms interchangeably because of his messianic world-
view of revolutionary activity.

Revolution for him was a mystical experience that allowed
him to perceive, and to participate in the march of history.
This was what he meant in the *Siete ensayos* when he developed the concept of indigenous socialism—a renewal—a return
to the ideal state of primitive communism. The same theme of
personal fulfillment, of self-realization through the participation in the transcendental march of history is carried forth in
the *Defensa del Marxismo*.

Mariátegui believed that the most evident effect of "parliamentarianism" was the psychological and intellectual resistance
of the leaders of the proletariat to the idea of the forcible seizure of political power. They were reluctant to take advantage
of the opportunity which history had thrust upon them during
the years of the Great War and the Bolshevik Revolution.
However, this crisis of revolutionary leadership ended with the
emergence of Lenin and the success of the Bolshevik Revolution.

While Mariátegui thought that Sorel had greatly influenced
Lenin's thought, he nevertheless believed that it was Lenin

who was the most energetic "restorer" of revolutionary Marxism. Indeed, he was the most prominent Marxist of the age. To Mariátegui, Lenin was the consummate political thinker and man of action.[3] It was he who had put into practice the violent passion (*pathos*), and the revolutionary emotion (*sentido*) which the Bernstein revisionists had ignored.[4] Lenin knew as Marx had known, that the conquest of political power was the basis for the creation of a new society based on the socialization of property. This was the great aim of Lenin's revolutionary activity.[5]

Despite this homage to Lenin, it was Georges Sorel who had the most profound influence on Mariátegui's thought. Sorel was more concerned with the spiritual or metaphysical aspects of Marxism. He returned to classical Marxism, voicing concern for the spiritual disequilibrium of the worker in a capitalist society. He tried to interpret the spiritual and moral world of the worker, his alienation from his work, and his powerlessness to effect any change of the social order.[6]

Sorel's concern for moral standards, and his conservative insistence on the value of tradition and customs in men's lives, paralleled basic and consistent themes in Mariátegui's own thought. Moreover, his apocalyptic view of revolution deeply influenced the Peruvian. For Mariátegui also held an eschatological view of a world that would be totally changed through spontaneous revolution. However, Mariátegui did differ from Sorel in one important respect: he firmly believed in the eventual triumph of the small band of revolutionaries, bound together in their great mission of igniting the spark of revolution. This was perhaps the only exclusively Leninist element that deeply influenced Mariátegui.

After a cursory treatment of the relationship of Marxism to Positivism and English political economy, Mariátegui compared the liberal and socialist economies. But he devoted more space to attacking the Bernstein "neo-revisionists" than to economic analysis. "Neo-revisionism," he wrote, "limits itself to a few superficial, empirical observations that do not explain the post-war crisis. The most important Marxist prediction— the capitalist concentration of wealth has occurred in the post-war era."[7] These "neo-revisionists" had abandoned the struggle for total and abrupt change of the economic and social order. In Mariátegui's view, they had become a part of the capitalist establishment.

Post-war capitalism had ceased to coincide with progress. The working class had lost its revolutionary drive, and had been deceived; it was now only concerned with the mundane issues of higher wages, better social services, and shorter work hours—all to be gained through parliamentary representation. Resurgent capitalism was merely concentrating economic and political power in the hands of a financial oligarchy. The "neo-revisionists" (Democratic Socialists) and their proletarian followers, were being bought off by capitalism's symbolic reforms and rewards.[8]

Mariátegui followed his economic analysis with a philosophical analysis of the "modern" Marxism of the post-war era. He related this modern Marxism to classical German philosophy, to the ideas of English political economy, and to French socialism. Very briefly, he traced Marxism and especially the concept of historical materialism up to the writings of Lenin. Quoting Benedetto Croce at almost every turn, Mariátegui stated that, "the transcendental dialectic of Kant precedes . . . the Marxist dialectic." Furthermore, "This materialist conception of Marx is born dialectically, as the antithesis of the idealist conception of Hegel."[9] What Mariátegui meant by this out of context re-hash of Croce was that Marx did not create history, but recognized and took advantage of the social and economic forces of history. Marx did not create socialism either; he merely interpreted the historical dialectic that pointed toward socialism.

Marxian socialism was not a classical philosophy according to Mariátegui; rather, it was a conception of the future condi-

tion of society. This conception, this ideal, had given hope to
the oppressed peoples of the world. Once they could understand
their condition and knew how to change that condition, they
were no longer at the mercy of their exploiters. They could
become masters of their own destiny, for they too could possess
the ideology and the faith that Mariátegui had acquired. Since
Marxism was a doctrine of hope it was not necessary that the
faithful understand its scientific philosophical ramifications.
The *idea* of the socialist society and the struggle to attain it
transcended all else.[10]

This "modern" Marxism far surpassed the other bankrupt
European philosophies—Neo-Thomism, Positivism and "Scientism." These philosophies were not doctrines of hope for
a better life since they were oriented toward the decadent past.
Neo-Thomism sought a return to feudal society, while Positivism and "Scientism," i.e., a blind faith in science and technolo-
gy, were the bulwarks of a resurgent, but doomed capitalism.
Mariátegui condemned traditional religions for their other-
worldly promise which had no scientific foundation. "The religion of the future [Marxism] will rest upon science, if any
belief has to rise to the category of a true religion."[11]

Marxism, in Mariátegui's view, combined the basic
strengths of both religion and science. It was scientific in that it
discovered and obeyed the laws of history. It was religious in
the sense that its adherents accepted those laws as a matter of
unquestioned faith. Furthermore, these believers earnestly
labored to fulfill the promise of the doctrine. "Some day,"
Mariátegui wrote wistfully, "the writings of Rosa Luxemburg
will evoke the same kind of devotion as those of Saint Teresa of
Ávila."[12]

Despite protestations to the contrary, Mariátegui's analysis
of "modern" Marxism returned time and time again to the
symbolic, and religiouslike aspects of the doctrine. His analytical guide, as he so often noted, was the "spirit," not the "letter" of Marxism. An essay that discussed the relationship of

ethics to socialism showed the Sorelian influence on Mariátegui even more clearly. He consistently maintained that Marxism was not an anti-ethical doctrine as some critics had argued. The fact that Marxism was founded on historical materialism did not make it unethical but scientific. The ethical *function* of Marxist socialism was not to be found in its philosophical speculations, but in its creation of a "moral de productores" (a proletarian ethic) for the struggle with the forces of capitalism.[13] This proletarian ethic emanated from the revolutionary aspirations of Marxism, and it was these aspirations that saved the proletariat from despair.[14]

The proletarian ethic had uplifted the workers and had given meaning to their lives once more. It ". . . freed them with an heroic heart, and a passionate will." Compromise was therefore unthinkable. For ". . . in order for the proletariat to fulfill its historic mission, its moral progress, it is necessary that it acquire a class consciousness. But this class consciousness in itself was not enough to bring about socialism. It must be wedded to a theory of revolutionary action as Lenin had so clearly stated."[15] Mariátegui viewed the struggle to achieve socialism as a self-cleansing process, a rebaptism that would somehow make men pure again. That struggle would *in itself* morally elevate workers and intellectuals. These revolutionaries, who were imbued with the selfless asceticism of socialism, would inevitably triumph over the materialistic greed of the capitalist system.[16]

Here Mariátegui introduced a whole new line of reasoning which can perhaps explain his indecisiveness about developing a formula for political action. An overview of his life and writings gives one the impression that he never really expected or intended his much heralded socialist society to ever come to pass. He seemed more content to place his revolutionary goal in the far-distant future. He never promised that a "new" Peru would take form during his lifetime. This may be due in part to his attachment to Marxism as a personal credo that could not be readily projected to others as a political doctrine. It may also be due to his firm belief that the very act of participation in bringing about socialism would itself be sufficient to raise the moral and ethical stature of the participants.

It was not of crucial importance, that everyone who participated in the revolutionary struggle adhere to a rigid Marxist line. As long as they worked for the same goals these "free spirits" could also share in the benefits of personal and moral elevation (a position that would lead Mariátegui to difficulties with the Comintern, and with those of his group who hewed to the Stalinist line).

The seemingly ambivalent attitude regarding the organization and direction of the revolutionaries had been a major factor in Mariátegui's split with Haya de la Torre and APRA. To Mariátegui, Haya was not interested in moral regeneration, only the capture of political power and its use. Mariátegui still held to the idea that an amorphous movement was the best way to gain adherents for the struggle. He was not ready to impose a rigid, specific ideology on his followers when he himself had none. Throughout his career, he repeatedly sought to avoid entanglement with a political party since he believed that the work of preparation had not proceeded far enough. If the *struggle alone* was sufficient to better man's moral nature, why then be so concerned about the specific means of conducting that struggle?

It was only in 1928 that Mariátegui, acceding to the wishes of some of his followers, agreed to create a political organization. The long-defunct Peruvian Socialist Party was re-organized under Mariátegui's leadership. This action was not so much due to any basic shift in Mariátegui's thought as it was to his declining health, the oppressive tactics of Leguía, and an overriding desire to prevent any further splintering of the revolutionaries in Peru.[17]

Despite the events of 1928 through 1930 that one might cite to disprove his contention, it is clear that Mariátegui's Marxism was not a formula for political action. It was a personal, religious-like code of ethics that enabled him to endure physical pain and psychological anguish. Through his Marxism, Mariátegui could become the "agonic soul" that Unamuno had so eloquently described. He could realize *himself* in a struggle that transcended the individual. It was a struggle for mankind. If one could summarize Mariátegui's revolutionary credo, it would be the following statement. "If socialism could not realize itself as a social order, this formidable work of education and elevation of mankind would be enough to justify its place in history."[18]

Mariátegui thought that the one thing that characterized the "modern" Marxism of the post-war era was the Marxist revolutionary's "heroic concept of life." Through the doctrine of revolutionary Marxism, man could once again feel that he could influence the social system—to establish a social order that would enable him to achieve his maximum self-realization. Mariátegui believed that since the founding of the Third International, Marxism had been given a new life, a new spirit. *Now* he wrote, the doctrine of Marx was infused ". . . with a mysticism very much like that of the catacombs of ancient Christianity."[19] The revolutionary Marxists were united in the pursuit of the common goal—socialism—and they now possessed the messianic fervor of the early Christian Church.

Mariátegui now introduced the question of the determinism of Marxist philosophy. "Marxism," he wrote, "where it has shown itself to be truly revolutionary—that is to say where it has been Marxist—has never obeyed a passive, rigid determinism."[20] He completely rejected the idea that Marxism was deterministic, and stated that it was the *only* modern doctrine that offered both a moral and political guide for man. Religions could not do this since they had become estranged from the historical and scientific experience of the nineteenth century. This was also true of Positivism—that "scientism" of blind faith in man's ability to achieve almost any desired result through the application of scientific method.

Marxism was the only doctrine that bridged the gap between man's historical experience and the modern scientific revolution. More importantly, Marxism filled the void in man's nature that had existed since the decline of religions. It was the only modern moral and ethical code that would enable men to once again control and order their own lives. Marxism had reversed the process of man's estrangement from his environment and from himself. Through Marxism, faith and science were combined for the general benefit of all mankind.[21]

The application of Marxist "scientific" principles was not merely blind obedience to a pre-ordained formula for social change, though Mariátegui did admit that the socialist tactic must conform to the historical situation. Actually, he never met this issue squarely but merely nibbled at the edges from time to time. He was so intent on denying the charge that Marxism was deterministic that he became hopelessly entangled in his own jargon, as the passage below indicates.

> The Marxist tactic is thus dynamic and dialectic as is the very doctrine of Marx; the socialist will not operate in a vacuum, does not disregard the pre-existing situation. . . . It conforms solidly to historical reality, but does not resign itself passively to it. Rather it reacts more energetically against it, in the sense of reinforcing the proletariat economically and spiritually, accentuating within it the consciousness of its conflict with the bourgeoisie, until having reached the fullest extent of their exasperation, and the bourgeoisie the full extent of the strength of the capitalist regime, converted into an obstacle to the productive forces, capitalism may be effectively overthrown, and substituted by a socialist regime with advantage for all. . . . each word, each action of Marxism has an accent of faith, of will, of heroic and creative conviction, whose impulse, it would be absurd to look for in a mediocre and passive determinist sentiment.[22]

Marxism was therefore not deterministic; it did not merely obey the forces of history, but took advantage of them. The revolutionary Marxist sought to move man to the next stage of history. His cause was absolutely pure and noble, since it was through the efforts of the revolutionary that mankind progressed, and the conflict of historical forces was resolved. Mankind benefited, not the revolutionary. In Mariátegui's view, the revolutionaries took advantage of historical forces in different ways and at different times. Their respective revolutions would correspond to the society, culture, and stage of development of their country. Marxism was a set of principles, a broad guideline for action. Therefore there was room for differing interpretations as long as they were Marxist *and* revolutionary, i.e., committed to basic social change.

Mariátegui saw the revolutionary struggle as basically a moral one. The revolutionaries represented the forces of Good, against the feudal and capitalist forces of Evil. His concern was for the humanistic side of the struggle and not the economic or political ends of that struggle. For Mariátegui, it was simply enough to believe that the Marxist revolutionary idea was a noble one. This led to all sorts of logical contradictions. The theoretical conception of Marxism—its economics and its theory of politics—was of less importance than the redemptive quality of the doctrine, as the following statement indicates.

> All . . . who proclaim a socialist ethic based on humanitarian principles, who do not work for the moral elevation of the proletariat are working unconsciously against their humanitarians . . . [He continued that Marx discovered and taught that one had to begin by understanding the fatality of the capitalist age, and above all its worth]. . . . [Furthermore] The proletariat succeeded the bourgeoisie in the civilizing mission. And it assumed its mission, conscious of its responsibility and capacity—acquired in the revolutionary activity, and in the capitalist factory—when the bourgeoisie fulfilled its destiny, it

ceased being a force of progress and culture. . . . [He concluded that] We Marxists do not believe that the task of creating a new order superior to the capitalist order, depends on an
amorphous mass of pariahs and oppressed led by evangelical
preachers of the good. The energy of revolution does not nour-
ish itself on compassion or envy. In the class struggle, wherein
reside all the elements of the sublime and the heroic . . . the
proletariat has to raise itself to an ethic of producers, far different and distinct from an ethic of slaves. . . .[23]

The above passages have been combined in an attempt to
show the inconsistency of Mariátegui's reasoning. Clearly he
was the very preacher of the good that he denounced. He
believed that he possessed the doctrine that would lead man to
a better life. Yet even if that better life were not realized during
his own time, the struggle in and of itself was worthwhile. The
revolutionaries would have still performed the noble task of
elevating their proletarian brethren to new heights of cultural
and moral perfection. (A position that Marx, and especially
Lenin would have denounced as mere petty-bourgeois senti-
mentality.)

Throughout his essays Mariátegui spared no effort in casti-
gating the "humanitarian reformers" who lacked an ideology
and a faith. Yet it is obvious that he himself lacked that clear
sense of purpose and direction that a political ideology could
provide. Once he had accepted Marxism as a *personal* metaphysical doctrine, he could not present it as a *political* one. Nor
could he ever follow a rigid doctrinal line that was laid down
by Lenin's successors. Mariátegui's uniquely personal Marxist
code was inadequate as the ideological guide for a revolutionary movement. This is perhaps one reason why the nationalism
of the *Siete ensayos* has had such a lasting impact in Peru,
while the Marxism of the *Defensa del Marxismo* has all but
vanished into oblivion.

As Mariátegui continued his essays on Marxism, it became
apparent that they were very subjective interpretations devoid

of any theoretical substance. Indeed, his analysis became more diffuse with each succeeding page. He thought that Marxism was the new doctrine of the future since it had acquired all of the élan of the old dogmas. Capitalism lacked ideological force; it could only counter the socialist argument with the private property principle, which he had previously demonstrated as being evil and decadent.[24]

Classical political economy according to Mariátegui was also incapable of opposing the arguments of Marxism. It was too utopian. Quoting Sorel, Mariátegui wrote that, "the Liberal political economy has been one of the best examples of a utopian society that one might cite. It imagined a society in which all would be reduced to commercial types, under the law of freest competition; it is now recognized today that this ideal society would be as difficult to achieve as that of Plato."[25]

Mariátegui conceded that Marx was probably correct in assuming that socialism could come about in England by peaceful means. But Mariátegui did not hold this hope for any other society, especially not Peru. He justified revolution with all of its violent implications by stating that the decadence and exhaustion of capitalism was not enough in itself to guarantee the ascension of socialism. Socialism was not the automatic consequence of capitalist decay, as the fascist "reaction" demonstrated. The Marxist revolutionaries had to take advantage of the opportunity that history presented to them, just as Lenin had done in Russia. They must seize the initiative from the forces of reaction in order to bring about the socialist society. Socialism, ". . . has to be the result of a tenacious and courageous work of ascension."[26]

Mariátegui never outlined in detail what this "courageous work of ascension" actually entailed. He provided some vague clues, all of which indicate that he like Sorel believed that revolution would occur *spontaneously*. Once the proletariat became aware of its historical mission, and was led by the inspiring example of the intellectual vanguard, the next stage of man's progress would automatically be achieved.[27] Everything hinged on the preparation of the revolutionary forces and on the correct interpretation of the proper point in time when the revolution would be successful. Mariátegui's only real concern was for the preparation of the revolution.

The determination of the proper time when the revolution would occur had been obliquely referred to throughout Mariátegui's Marxist essays. All depended on the state of exhaustion of capitalism. Capitalism was not only becoming bankrupt as an economic system, it was also crumbling as an ideal and a philosophy. This was evidence by the decadence of its arts and letters, In an essay on "Materialist Idealism," Mariátegui lamented the "spiritualization" of Marxism by intellectuals, stating that he himself had suffered from this "malady" in his early exposure to Marx.[28] Capitalism he argued, had renounced its own liberal philosophy, and like the decadent civilization of Rome, ". . . looked for a narcotic in Oriental and Asian metaphysics."[29]

The thrust of this attack on capitalist art and letters was directed mainly at the Modernists. Modernism was a literary movement that dominated French and Hispanic literature during Mariategui's time, and he viewed the movement as the epitome of capitalist decadence in literature. The Modernists rejected the social and political realities of their age and cultivated a philosophy of "art for art's sake." Their literary production was addressed to a very limited audience of "aesthetes." It was characterized by eroticism, escapism in oriental forms, and allegory, and made a fetish of the cult of the artificial in literature.

In Mariátegui's view, non-Marxist intellectuals had abdicated their responsibility as intellectuals for they were unconcerned politically, and were unwilling to take up their historic task as revolutionary leaders. The Marxists in contrast, were fulfilling their historic mission. And what is more, their doctrine was pure. Mariátegui wrote that, ". . . the greatest sign of the health and power of socialism, as a principle of a new civilization, will undoubtedly be its resistance to all of these spiritualist ecstacies."[30] Just as socialism would supplant capitalism as a political and economic order, so would it surpass capitalism in the realm of art, literature, and speculative philosophy. This was inevitable, since Marxism was the only philosophy that was truly based on the intellectual and philosophical heritage of the West.[31]

Mariátegui believed that the time was ripe to mobilize youth in the struggle to achieve socialism. This mobilization would take full account of the idealism and boundless energies of youth. But it would strengthen that idealism and harness those energies through the doctrine of Marxism.

> A messianic and romantic sentiment, more or less widespread in the intellectual youth of the post-war generation, that inclines it to an excessive idea which is at times delirious, influences this youth to find Marxism more or less behind the times with respect to the needs of this "new sensibility." In politics as in literature, there is real substance in this term. But this does not hinder "the new sensibility," which in the social and ideological order prefers to call itself the "new spirit," from coming close to making a true myth, whose real evaluation, whose strict analysis, it is time to undertake without opportunist caution.[32]

His essay continued in the same vein, but with greater clarity when he wrote that, "what interests us now in these critical times of capitalist stabilization and the factors that prepare for a new revolutionary offensive, is not so much the psychoanalysis or the idealization of the juvenile passion of 1919 [i.e., the University Reform Movement], as the clarifying of those values it created and the experience that it has provided."[33] Mariátegui saw that the propensity of youth to form a romantic attachment to any new cause was one of its great weaknesses as a revolutionary force. Youth did not possess the sense of dedication and discipline that was based on a firm ideology. As such, it was an utterly unstable, and unreliable revolutionary ally. This was his basic argument against those who would "spiritualize" Marxism. (Yet he himself had "spiritualized" the doctrine by making it a personal credo.)

Mariátegui wanted to explain and interpret emotions of youth. He had seen in Italy (and in Peru) what could happen if these energies were not channelled toward concrete goals. "The word youth has been compromised," he wrote. And he cited the Giovinezza movement of Fascist Italy as an example of what could happen to a youth movement without an ideology.* The ideals and energies of youth could be harnessed by the forces of reaction.[34] Mariátegui implied that this was what had also occurred in Peru when the University Reform Movement had been almost totally absorbed into the APRA of Haya de la Torre.

The first decades of the twentieth century had seen the collapse of the revolutionary solidarity of the socialists. This, thought Mariátegui, was due to the rise of democratic socialism and fascism. This unity, however, was being restored by the "modern" Marxists. This new generation could be the catalyst that would unite youth behind the "true" socialist cause. Mere youthful protest and rebellion were not enough to change the social structure. Mariátegui's great hope for the success of his revolution lay in preparing another generation for the continuing struggle to achieve socialism. "Until now," he wrote, "the triumphant abstraction of the revolution of '19 amounts to very little in history, when compared to the concrete work of the positive creation of the U.S.S.R."[35]

The examples of the leaders of the Third International were those that should appeal to youth. The Marxism of Lenin,

*The Giovinezza movement was an Italian youth movement that militated for change in Italy. The movement had been captured by the Fascists for their own purposes.

Stalin, and Trotsky was the true guide for the "new generation." "The conquest of youth," he continued, "cannot cease to
be, however, one of the most evident and actual necessities of
the revolutionary parties. But on the condition that youth may
know, that tomorrow it will fall to their lot to fulfill their revolutionary mission without the alibis of youth, with the responsibility and capacity of men."[36]

In his remaining essays, Mariátegui concentrated on com-
paring the "true revisionists" with Marx and Engels. Lenin's
great success as a revolutionary thinker and man of action, was
described as, ". . . his facility to continue his work of criticism
and preparation, without ever relaxing his determination after
the debacle of 1905."[37] Lenin had continued that great work of
Marx and Engels by combining criticism and revolutionary
preparation, with revolutionary *action.* Here Mariátegui
tried to justify his work of preparation and his relative inaction
as a leader. "The great value of the work of Marx and
Engels," he wrote, "was spiritual and scientific, and this is
quite independent of its revolutionary efficacy, . . . they were
the first *in not considering the imminence of insurrection."*
[Italics added.] "Analysis did not inhibit action, nor action the
analysis."[38]

Mariátegui had by this time succeeded in impaling himself
on the horns of a dilemma of his own creation. He had attacked
those who would "spiritualize" Marxism. Yet in this essay, he
stated that the spiritual element of Marxism was one of its
main assets. He seemed only concerned with interpreting history and preparing for revolution. Yet he had actually developed a program of endless "analysis, criticism, and preparation." His was becoming a static doctrine—of knowing when
not to move. Mariátegui did not possess those rare attributes of
leadership and sense of timing that made political theorists
political men of action.

The essays concluded with an attack on those intellectuals
who had no political orientation. Intellectuals were skeptical of

any ideological view of the world, afraid to make a commitment. They distrusted the inherent good in man. Therefore
they could not communicate with men or influence men's
actions. Mariátegui stated that intellectuals were impeded in
any attempt to institute social change since they rejected dogmatism, *i.e.,* a doctrinal world-view. He concluded that, "A
dogmatist like Marx or Engels influences events more than any
great heretic or nihilist."[39] Mariátegui loathed the non-political
intellectual—types with which he probably had associated
while living in Paris. For Mariátegui *all* activity was political;
everything else was meaningless.

Several threads run through these essays on Marxism. We
have seen, for instance, that Mariátegui thought that the goals
of revolutionary activity had been set down by Marx for all to
see. But Marx had not prescribed the specific *kind* of revolutionary activity that would be applicable to each society's quest
for the socialist ideal. Mariátegui believed that it was up to the
post-war generation of Marxists to adapt Marxism to particular historical and cultural situations. He derived his sense of
direction and purpose from the writings of Sorel, just as he
thought Lenin had done. Marxism was Mariátegui's "com-
pass" for the revolutionary journey; it provided a general sense
of direction for his political course.[40] In his view, the modern
Marxist revolutionary accepted the premises of Marx, while
developing the doctrine to fit new contexts. He stated that,
"Sorel succeeded in an original continuation of Marxism
because he began by accepting all of the premises of Marxism,
not by repudiating them a priori, and *en masse.* . . . Lenin
proves to us with the unimpeachable testimony of successful
revolution, that Marxism is the only way of continuing and
going beyond Marx."[41]

This interpretation of Marxism was not unique in the
1920's. Many intellectuals bent on changing their societies
were attracted to the doctrine as the great hope for mankind.
Many, however, were disillusioned by the end of the 1920's.

After the death of Lenin, and the exile of Trotsky, Stalin emerged as the leader of the world socialist revolution and individual, or nationalist, interpretations of Marxism were no longer tolerated. Nationalism was downgraded as an ally of the socialist revolutionaries. Those who adhered to the Third International (including Mariátegui) were expected to follow the dictates of the newly formed Communist International (Comintern). Many, like Mariátegui, who adhered to the "spirit" rather than the "letter" of Marxism, had to either quit the movement or submit to the ideological and political control of the Moscow-based Comintern.

Since Mariátegui's belief was so much a part of his psychological make-up he could never change that belief to suit the shifting interpretations of "correct" Marxism that emerged from the Comintern. He never altered his own personal belief system and consequently he could never alter his political beliefs either. As the Latin American Communist parties were organized in the late 1920's, Mariátegui's interpretation of Marxism became quite distinct from that of the Communists. Splits occurred among his followers, and it was becoming evident that he was losing control of his movement. None disputed his basically nationalist position regarding "Peruvian reality," even though his *Siete ensayos* were tinged with a Marxism that was by 1928 heretical. Mariátegui's Marxism was an expression of a personal belief, and as such it was difficult to project that belief as a political ideology. He encountered this difficulty when he attempted to found a Marxist political party.

In 1928, he presided over the founding of the new Peruvian Socialist Party. He had less than two years to live, and there was still much to be done. His founding of the Socialist Party was an attempt to move from the realm of theory, to the operationalization of that theory. The successes and failures of this last stage of Mariátegui's career are the subject of the following chapter.

9

The Years of Despair
1928–1930

The seventeenth number of *Amauta,* as we have seen, signalled a definite shift in Mariátegui's approach to socialist revolution in Peru. In the lead article, "Anniversary and Balance," he wrote that the work of *ideological definition* had been completed. It was now time to begin the "heroic" creation of socialism in Peru.[1]

Perhaps the most important determinant of this new course was the break-up of the left-wing revolutionaries. By 1928 the movement was irreparably splintered; Mariátegui and Haya de la Torre were no longer fighting for control of the same movement. Rather, they represented two distinct approaches to social revolution. While they competed for the allegiance of the same groups to build their respective political organizations, they had clearly opposite approaches to the direction and purpose of social revolution. Ideologically, they both drew upon the ideas of González Prada and Marx. They believed that an alliance of intellectuals, urban workers, and the ubiquitous Indian masses was the correct strategy for revolution in Peru. Their great differences were over the organization of these groups into a political party, the composition of party leadership, and the tactics that the party should follow.

Prior to 1928 Mariátegui had been skeptical about the usefulness of forming a political party. He still thought in terms of creating an amorphous movement, guided by a universalistic ideology and open to all who opposed the semi-feudal, bourgeois order. His writings up to September of 1928 indicated that he was still engaged in an apparently endless task of "criticism and definition." His experience in Europe made him. cautious about organizing for political action without first having clearly determined the ends for which that action was intended. Without a clear sense of purpose and direction, political action could result in fascist reaction. He saw this as the great danger of Haya de la Torre's APRA, the founding of which seemed premature. Still, as late as 1927 Mariátegui gave APRA his "support in principle."

This tacit support faded as Mariátegui's ideological position hardened. He believed that Haya's "alliance," his Frente Único, was becoming a political party rather than a movement. Moreover, Mariátegui thought that Haya de la Torre was exhibiting the dangerous fascist tendency of seeking to convert his organization into a vehicle for the pursuit of personal power. Several factors led him to this conclusion: APRA did not have a dogmatic and all-inclusive ideology that was a bulwark against personalism. Furthermore, the APRA leader wanted Mariátegui to join *his* group, but only as a subordinate not a co-equal. Mariátegui would have to submit to the direction of another. No longer would he be able to maintain ideological purity, or political independence.[2] This was clearly unacceptable to Mariátegui.

In the spring of 1928 the dispute between Peru's two great revolutionary leaders widened to include the Peruvian political exiles. These political dissidents were living in exile in Paris, Mexico City, La Paz, Havana, and Buenos Aires. Most of these groups were followers of Haya de la Torre. When he founded APRA in 1924, they organized themselves into *aprista* cells. Yet most of the exiles had "fraternal" bonds with Mariátegui. They were soon brought into the polemic through letters that Haya and Mariátegui wrote to them, seeking their support in the struggle for leadership.

Haya never understood Mariátegui's position about the difference between a movement and political party. He thought

Mariátegui, ". . . absurdly sentimental and guilty of engaging in useless semantics." He wrote that, "APRA is a party, an alliance, and a front at the same time." He continued by accusing Mariátegui of viewing the Latin American political situation through European eyes. He implied that Mariátegui was incapable physically and intellectually, of any kind of dynamic political leadership.[3] (Perhaps he was correct in this respect. Mariátegui's failing health, his poor speaking ability, and his penchant for long ideological digressions did not evoke the kind of mass loyalty and enthusiasm that Haya could generate.)

Mariátegui had been willing to support the APRA as long as it was clearly understood that it was only a part of the Peruvian movement for social revolution. Once it became clear that its leader thought it to be the *only true* revolutionary movement, Mariátegui withdrew his tacit support. Given his tendency to see the revolutionary struggle as worldwide, it is not surprising that Mariátegui would distrust a movement that appeared to be merely hemispheric, or even national in scope. By 1928 he was firmly convinced that APRA was going the same route as the Kuomintang in China. It was moving from a socialist to a nationalist, and finally to a personalistic fascist movement. It had no firm ideological base, and was therefore opportunistic. This was its greatest weakness. It was also its greatest threat to those who wanted to bring about a socialist revolution in Peru.

As soon as Haya learned of Mariátegui's criticisms, especially regarding APRA's lack of ideology, he accused Mariátegui of being a Communist who took direct orders from Moscow. Not only was he dancing to a tune called in Moscow, but he was also collaborating with Leguía at the same time so as to undermine APRA's influence.[4] The accusations were patently absurd. But in this struggle for political survival no quarter was given, especially by Haya de la Torre. He was working at a serious disadvantage, for he too was in exile. Meanwhile Mariátegui commanded the polemical heights in Lima.

The dispute had forced Mariátegui to consider the need to create a political counterpoise to APRA if Peru was to follow a Marxist revolutionary path. Some of his more militant followers also urged him to consider a more active political course. Mariátegui had always avoided the entanglements of leading a political organization, but the pressures from his followers, his declining health, and the bitter polemic with APRA moved him toward the kind of political activity that he had always avoided. Another factor that nudged him a bit further along this path was his fear that the forces of fascist reaction were gaining momentum in his own hemisphere.

Mariátegui believed that even the great Mexican Revolution was entering into a Thermidorian stage. In Mexico, the ruling party (Partido Nacional Revolucionario or PNR) was reaching a collaborationist detent with the forces of feudal and bourgeois reaction, namely the Catholic Church and the United States government.[5] APRA also advocated this dangerous course, especially cooperation with the bourgeoisie. It was a party that allied itself with the bourgeoisie. Mariátegui concluded that APRA was *not* revolutionary, for such an alliance ". . . was the very basis of *Leguísmo*."[6] He made this quite clear in a statement that summarized the ideological position of his newly emerging Socialist Party.

The peasants' demands did not triumph against feudalism in Europe as long as they expressed themselves in "jacqueries." They triumphed with the liberal, bourgeois revolution which transformed those demands into a program. In our still semi-feudal Spanish America the bourgeoisie has not cared, nor has it known how to fulfill the task of the liquidation of feudalism. . . . Socialism takes up this task. The socialist doctrine is the only one that can give a modern, constructive meaning [*sentido*] to the indigenous cause . . . the realization of this task is dependent on the will and the discipline of a class that today makes its appearance in our historical process; the proletariat.[7]

The proletariat needed the guidance, and the heroic leadership of the small band of elite revolutionaries. Without this direction by "the vanguard of the proletariat," the socialist revolution was doomed to failure.[8] Somewhat reluctantly, Mariátegui finally decided to lend his prestige, and his dwindling physical energies to the new task of founding a truly socialist and revolutionary party in Peru.

The Fall of 1928 was a period of feverish activity among the *mariáteguistas* in Lima as they prepared for the re-founding of the Peruvian Socialist Party (PSP). The first cell meeting of the PSP was held in Lima on September 16th of that year. Significantly, Mariátegui was unable to attend due to his poor health. The meeting like many that followed, was chaired by his second-in-command, Ricardo Martínez de la Torre. The founding of the PSP, which coincided with the new tone and direction of *Amauta,* made public the irreparable split among the revolutionaries. From that time on, Mariátegui and his group bitterly opposed APRA, ". . . that . . . idea of a petty-bourgeois, and demagogic nationalist party."[9]

By the late 1920's there were three distinct positions taken by left-wing revolutionaries in Peru. These were discussed at great length at the first plenary session of the PSP. First there was Haya de la Torre's position: his revolutionary formula was based on the Frente Único idea of the early 1920's. This consisted of an alliance of the four major revolutionary groups in Peru: urban workers, intellectuals, Indian peasants, and the "revolutionary" elements of the national bourgeoisie. It was the presence of this latter group in Haya's "alliance" that caused the dispute with those who viewed a Peruvian social revolution in a strictly Marxist context. A second position was held by members of Mariátegui's own group, but not by Mariátegui himself. This was advanced most notably by Martínez de la Torre, Eudocio Ravines, Hugo Pesce, and Julio Portocarrero. It called for the immediate organization by hard-core

Communists—absolutely no bourgeois elements were to be admitted.

The third position was advanced by Mariátegui; and it became the formula for the founding of the PSP. Mariátegui called for the organization of a Peruvian Socialist Party rather than a narrow-based Communist organization. The PSP was to be open to all who wanted to work for the revolutionary cause. It was still "an alliance of free spirits" but Mariátegui held to the Leninist concept that the PSP should be guided by a small elite of dedicated Marxist revolutionaries—though not necessarily avowed Communists.

The PSP structure resembled a series of concentric circles; all direction was to emanate from the center of other groups in the party (labor unions, student associations, and Indian communities). Alliance and cooperation with the bourgeoisie *as a class* was unthinkable, but individual members of that class could enter the party and eventually move toward the center as they became more Marxist oriented. The party was avowedly international, but only in its socialist label. It was theoretically in step with the world revolutionary movement through its association with the Third International (with which it became affiliated in 1928). In every other respect it clearly resembled a nationalist party.

Mariátegui was firmly convinced of the correctness of the Leninist interpretation of Marx's *Communist Manifesto*— that the great struggle between the proletariat and the bourgeoisie was first a national struggle. The proletariat of each country must first settle matters with its own bourgeoisie before proceeding to build socialism. Mariátegui thought that APRA was not a revolutionary party, since it was not concerned with this central question. Moreover, as a diffuse continental movement its chances for success in Peru were seriously diminished. This conviction of Mariátegui's was "correct" in the days of Lenin—an example of the congruence of Mariátegui's and the

communist ideas propounded by Lenin. But it led to difficulty
with the Stalinist-dominated Comintern. Nationalism by 1928
had become suspect as a reliable revolutionary ally of the world
socialist revolution.[10]

The PSP program was officially adopted by the party leadership at a meeting held on October 7, 1928. It clearly bore the
stamp of Mariátegui's influence, but also reflected an attempt
to keep movement from any further splits. Shorn of hyperbole
and Marxist jargon, the program read like an essay from the
González Prada era.[11]

The program was clearly not that of a communist party,
indeed it was quite similar to the APRA program that was
adopted in the early 1930's. Mariátegui called for a party
directed by an elite, which would follow the organization and
tactics of Leninist class warfare. Yet Peru had no well defined,
modern class structure, as Mariátegui himself admitted in his
Siete ensayos. The proletarian base of his party was indeed
small and weak; it could not number more than a few hundred
thousand members out of a total population of some eight million. Haya de la Torre obviously understood this weakness in
Mariátegui's position—his accusation that Mariátegui was
attempting to impose a European model of social revolution on
Peru had a certain ring of truth about it. With the promulga-
tion of the Socialist Party's program, Mariátegui declared
himself in open conflict with APRA, and with the Leguía
regime as well.

Throughout the decade of the 1920's the Leguía government
had preserved itself by keeping opposing forces off balance. The
remarkable durability of the diminutive president was not due
to the firm backing of any of the traditional institutional props
that buttressed governments in Peru. Instead, Leguía's longev-
ity depended on the post-war boom in world commodity prices,
and the huge foreign investments in mining and industry.
Economic conditions were such that the landowners were content, while the fat on the economy allowed Leguía to buy off

the military with increased salaries, perquisites, and new equipment.

Leguía's plan for economic development was to build an economic infrastructure (transportation, communication, power facilities, and an irrigation system). This was to be the prelude to industrialization. In order to accomplish this, his government offered concessions to foreign investors that would aid the development of these vital sectors. This policy led to the charge by Mariátegui and other left-wing leaders, that the wealth of the nation was being mortgaged in perpetuity to foreign interests. (Today, some avowedly leftist intellectuals privately admit that the economic progress achieved by Leguía was a positive factor in Peru's present-day economic development.)

Throughout the *oncenio* large sums accrued to the state treasury. However, much of it had to be spent to redeem Peru's long-standing international debts and to keep the army in its barracks. By 1929 though, the economic policy of the Leguía government was being seriously questioned. The economic boom was coming to a rapid end; and business groups and the military were becoming increasingly restive. The army in particular, was moving from its position of aloofness as it became more apprehensive about its position as the traditional arbiter of the political life of the nation.[12]

The emergence of fascism in Europe and the condition of the deteriorating Peruvian economy constituted the second set of factors that convinced Mariátegui that the time was propitious for the organization of a Socialist Party. Most Marxists tended to see the deepening world economic depression as a force that would produce a more intensive imperialist drive. Therefore, if the Marxist revolutionary did not prepare for the new era, the revolutionary opportunity would be lost. The initiative would then pass on to the forces of fascist reaction which seemed to be on the march everywhere.[13]

Mariátegui's interpretation of this situation, and his attacks on APRA drew a bitter response from Haya de la Torre.

Mariátegui thinks like an intellectual of the period when he was in Europe. . . . . My fraternal objections to Mariátegui were always against his lack of a sense of realism, against his excessive intellectualism, and his almost total lack of understanding of the efficacy of efficient action. . . . . Mariátegui is immobilized and his work is merely intellectual. To us who are in action falls the task of seeing reality face to face, and of dealing with it. In our environment only action shows the way to revolution. . . . . He cringes from the idea of action. He is an intellectual. He will say as Plekhanov, the great Russian Marxist teacher of Lenin, 'but if it is revolution it is not the Marxist revolution.' . . . . Thus speaks Plekhanov and all the intellectuals. . . .[14]

The APRA leader refused to enter into any kind of alliance with Mariátegui's Socialist Party, stating that APRA was hemispheric while the PSP merely national. He accused Mariátegui of waging a "divisionist campaign," and he belittled him as a mere "Lima Socialist" whose organization was a cover for the penetration of Peru by the Third International.[15]

Once it became known that Mariátegui had organized a political party, some Peruvians in exile began to line up behind him. In Paris a cell of the PSP was organized *within* the existing APRA cell. (The Paris cell of APRA completely dissolved in 1929.) In La Paz the APRA cell went over entirely to Mariátegui. The Mexican group, with few defections, remained loyal to Haya de la Torre. These developments had undoubtedly been influenced by the course of the world communist movement in the late 1920's. Indeed, some of the key members of the Central Committee of the Peruvian Socialist Party were avowed Communists (Eudocio Ravines, Julio Portocarrero, and Hugo Pesce).

There is some evidence suggesting that the Communists were interested in capitalizing on Mariátegui's popularity in order to build a Communist organization with some mass appeal. Moscow had completely changed its attitude about nationalist parties; and this attitude was reflected in the arguments of the Communists of the Central Committee of the PSP. Nationalist parties were no longer viewed as they were in Lenin's time, as allies in the struggle for socialism. Stalin, who bitterly recalled what had happened when the Communists collaborated with the Kuomintang, now ruled the U.S.S.R. No cooperation with the national bourgeoisie was permitted. Moreover, all parties adhering to the Third International were to submit to central control of the Comintern. These local Communist parties were soon subordinated to the Stalinist strategy of building socialism in one country—the Soviet Union.

The Communists saw APRA as an obstacle to any penetration of Peru. Mariátegui's group on the other hand, gave them reason to hope that the nascent Peruvian Socialist Party could be the base for a Peruvian Communist Party. Perhaps even Mariátegui could be converted as had his mentor Henrí Barbusse. Initially, the Communists believed that they could work through Mariátegui. Throughout 1928 Comintern agents tried to persuade him to transform the PSP into a Communist Party. The most active of these agents were the members of the PSP Central Committee, Julio Portocarrero, and Eudocio Ravines.[16] Mariátegui adamantly refused to permit the PSP to be designated as a Communist Party, or even a first step in the formation of a Communist organization. He refused to submit to Comintern dictates even though he had taken his party into the Third International. His reasons for wanting to head an independent party had been clearly stated in his dispute with Haya de la Torre; and no doubt they were the same regarding the Communists. In addition, the Comintern was an international agent of the Soviet Union and Mariátegui wanted no ties with a movement that was directed from outside Peru.

Despite Mariátegui's protestations, the Communists viewed the PSP as merely a transitional organization that would one day become a Communist one.[17] The Communists have since obscured these facts by trying to claim Mariátegui as their

martyred founder and leader. But a careful study of Mariátegui's statements indicates that he had no intention of permit-
ting the PSP to fall under Communist control.[18] Furthermore,
a study of the letters and documents indicates that by 1929 the
Comintern and its agents had abandoned their efforts to convert Mariátegui to their cause. They could never be certain of
his reliability, nor of his willingness to carry out Comintern
directives.

Since the rise of Stalin, a campaign had been underway to
make local Communist parties more amenable to Moscow.
Original theoretical contributions to Marxist-Leninist thought
were viewed with suspicion as the parties entered into a period
of bureaucratization. Moscow now began to attack Mariátegui
as a petty-bourgeois reformer; and it further sought to discredit
him by accusing him of the high crime of "Trotskyism." Mariátegui finally decided to answer these charges at a forthcoming
meeting in Buenos Aires. Since his dispute with APRA, Mariátegui had apparently been pushed further and further along the
path of sharpening his ideas on the implementation of revolutionary Marxism. The Buenos Aires meeting was his last hesitant step in this direction.[19]

The First Latin American International Communist Congress met in the Spring of 1929. (Its official designation according to the minutes of the meeting was the Congreso Socialista
de Latinoamerica.)[20] Some thirty-eight delegates met to begin
the process of organizing the Communist parties in Latin America in accordance with the latest directives from Moscow. In
attendance were representatives from North and South America, France, and the Soviet Union.

Stalin, through the Comintern, had ordered that under no
circumstances should there be any cooperation with the
national bourgeosie. Nor was there to be any variation of party
organization, structure, or tactics to fit differing political or
cultural circumstances. More importantly, no independent
interpretations of Marxist-Leninist doctrine were to be

permitted—all doctrinal pronouncements were to originate from Moscow.

The delegates lost no time in branding the APRA as a Latin American Kuomintang. Open warfare was declared on Haya de la Torre and his organization—the goal was the complete destruction of APRA. Mariátegui did not attend the conference due to his tubercular condition; however, it is quite likely that he would have supported the resolutions against APRA. Following this initial display of unanimity the Congress got down to the problem of Mariátegui. There the unity vanished and the remaining sessions were spent in acrimonious debate.

The chief critic of Mariátegui was the Comintern representative for Latin America who called himself "Luis" (quite likely his real name was Victor Codovilla). He objected to Mariátegui's argument regarding the need for preparation of the masses for revolution, and that until such preparations were complete, the formation of a Communist party would be of little utility. Luis argued that this was bad thinking and smacked of "possibilism" and he further argued that the founding of a socialist party would create *two* mutually competitive parties. He stated that the PSP was a multi-class party and that therefore, it suffered from the same ideological and organizational defects as the APRA. The Comintern representative concluded by stating that only a truly proletarian party led by a small dedicated Communist elite could succeed.

The Peruvian "question" broke the Congress wide open since it involved the issue of Mariátegui's credibility as a Marxist revolutionary. The struggle between the Communists and Mariátegui was not a unique one in this period when Moscow was trying to re-orient its thinking about the "national question." However, in Latin America the national question became a racial one at the Congress. Here the delegates wrestled with the problem of defining the role of the masses of Indians in the making of a proletarian revolution. Was the Indian a proletarian or a peasant? And if he were a peasant, what was his role in a proletarian party? The question was discussed at great length, and ended with the reading of Mariátegui's paper on the races *(El problema de las razas en América Latina)*, and their vital role as a revolutionary base.

According to one account, the Congress had no interest whatsoever in Mariátegui's views on the Indian question. Nor was it interested in defining the Indian's role in the coming socialist revolution. Its sole objective was to extend the bureaucratic control of the Comintern over the emerging Latin American Communist parties.[21] It might be added that the only Communist parties that followed the Moscow line were those of the racially homogeneous countries of Chile, Uruguay, and Argentina. The Communists, by failing to deal with the racial question, i.e., "the national question," found themselves at a serious disadvantage in those countries with large Indian populations that could be drawn into non-Communist nationalist movements.

Mariátegui's adamant refusal to found a Communist party posed a serious obstacle to Communist penetration of Peru. The International Congress, which convened to create unity among the Latin American parties, adjourned with the delegates in greater disarray than ever. Moreover, a serious split with Mariátegui had developed. Mariátegui was finally rebuked by the Congress for his nationalist and "Trotskyite" views. His paper on the races was summarily brushed aside. But he still was too popular a figure to be read out of the movement just yet; an open break with Mariátegui had to be avoided at all costs. For the time being at least, he still commanded great respect among Marxists throughout the hemisphere. It was finally decided that the only way to deal with him would be to discredit him, to undermine his stature so that he would lose his position of prestige in Latin America.

Following the last session of the Congress, "Luis" wrote to Moscow for instructions on how to deal with Mariátegui. The answer came in a roundabout way to Hugo Pesce and Julio

Portocarrero. In January of 1930, a letter arrived from Moscow directing these two to begin the organization of a Peruvian Communist Party despite Mariátegui's opposition. Eudocio Ravines was sent from Paris to Lima to insure compliance with these instructions and to attempt to undermine Mariátegui's influence within the PSP. Here the accounts become extremely difficult to follow. Ricardo Martínez de la Torre asserts that the Peruvian Communist Party was organized in September of 1928, and that he himself led the organizational meeting. Ravines stated that the Communist Party was not organized until *after* Mariátegui's death which was April, 1930. He asserts that the Peruvian Communist Party emerged from a split in the then leaderless PSP. Martínez de la Torre's account attempts to prove that Mariátegui was an avowed Communist *before* his death. It would appear that the facts have been altered to fit Martínez de la Torre's account. Informants generally acknowledged that Ravines was the actual founder of the Peruvian Communist Party. Though he is no longer a Communist, Ravines himself acknowledged this. His account seems more in accord with the evidence uncovered.[22]

In March of 1930, a meeting of the Central Committee of the PSP was presided over by Mariátegui. By this time he was but a mere shadow of his old self. The repercussions of the International Congress had already been felt in Peru, and a split had developed among his inner circle. Some wanted to organize a Communist Party immediately, while others followed Mariátegui who still clung to his original position. Letters had been received from exiled followers of Mariátegui that accused him of trying to dodge the whole issue. Only he himself could resolve the dispute and perhaps heal the schism.

For some unexplained reason Mariátegui never met this issue squarely and the meeting ended in a complete deadlock.[23] By this time, his illness was in the terminal stage. Quite likely he simply did not have the energy to deal with yet another schism. However, immediately after his death, a letter was sent

from Comintern Headquarters in Buenos Aires urging the
Mariátegui group to immediately form a Communist Party.[24]
On May 20, 1930, just one month after the death of their
revered leader, the Central Committee of the PSP met at Chos-
ica. Twelve members adopted a resolution which changed the
name of the PSP and its program as well. Only Martínez de la
Torre, by his own account, voiced opposition. Thus the organization that Mariátegui founded with the great hope of making
a truly Peruvian social revolution, became the Peruvian
Communist Party and a mere tool of the Comintern.

10

MARIÁTEGUI'S LEGACY

On April 16, 1930, Mariátegui died at the age of thirty-five. His death was the signal for a great outpouring of emotion. On Good Friday April 18, a procession passed from the Mariátegui home through the narrow streets of downtown Lima to the Cementerio General. The bier, carried by his closest friends, was draped with a red flag. Thousands of mourners bearing flowers and placards followed singing the *Internationale*. President Leguía must have felt uneasy as the cortege wound its way through the Plaza de Armas and past the presidential palace. At the cemetery a marathon of eulogies lasted until dark. Then the casket was lowered with all those present vowing eternal fealty to Mariátegui's revolutionary cause.[1]

This event saw the end of an era in Peru—an era of romantic revolutionary fervor. After Mariátegui's death the bitterness of his disputes with APRA and the Communists was temporarily forgotten. He was praised by all as a ". . . symbol of the new Peruvian generation, an apostle of a new Peruvian age."[2] This sentiment has not diminished over the years, at least among his surviving followers. One of them, Martin Adán stated: "Mariátegui was about as warm personally as a mathematician. But he was truly sensitive about the feelings of others. He succeeded in awakening an entire generation of intellectuals; and we still feel his presence."[3]

Mariátegui's body was barely in the grave before the struggle for his mantle began. Each disputant claimed that *he alone* was the "true" follower of Mariátegui's doctrine. Indeed, this dispute has continued in Peru to this day; and it revolves around the "correct" interpretation of Mariátegui's revolutionary thought and program for action.

There is a romantic aura that surrounds Mariátegui's legacy in modern Peru. He remains the epitome of Unamuno's "agonic soul." His psychological struggles, physical pain, and untimely death have combined to lend a certain mystical quality to his ideas. Yet these factors have also contributed to obscuring the nature of those ideas. Mariátegui has been praised and condemned as a socialist, a communist, a populist reformer, and a messianic nationalist. He was probably a bit of all these stereotypes. But above all, Mariátegui looms as *the* major force in the development of twentieth century Peruvian nationalism, or *peruanidad* as it is now termed. It is this nationalism or peruanidad that remains the major ideological force in the Peruvian political process.

The deification of Mariátegui has been most obvious in the writings of the Communists. He has become for them an infinitely more valuable figure dead than he ever was alive. (His valuable personal papers have all disappeared.) After his death his small library was sold by his widow to the University of San Marcos. Most of this collection has since been lost. Mariátegui's private papers were confiscated by the police and have never been recovered. The Communists repeatedly have attempted to link Mariátegui to their cause; even though available evidence refutes this connection. Communist accounts claim him as their revered founder and martyred apostle. Party membership cards have carried his picture; and at party meetings Mariátegui is displayed alongside Marx and Lenin. Had he lived longer, it is likely that he would have allied with Haya de la Torre in opposing Communist penetration of Peru in the 1930's. For at the time of his death, he was just beginning to perceive the threat that the Communists posed to any truly *national* revolution in Peru.

The elements of Marxism and Peruvian nationalism in

Mariátegui's thought have been selectively chosen as his
"true" theories on revolution by "successors" of every ideological leaning. Indeed, had the Communists succeeded in becoming a major force in Peruvian politics, it is likely that
Mariátegui would be revered as a Communist rather than a
nationalist. However, Peruvian politics has been dominated
by nationalist reform groups instead of the Communists.
(Quite likely this was due to the failure of the Communists
to deal with the "national question.") Because of this, Mariátegui has become the pre-eminent theorist of Peruvian nationalism. He is remembered as a nationalist instead of a Marxist
theoretician.

We know that Mariátegui's view of social change (revolución) was a process of continuous individual moral and
spiritual regeneration. Yet there is little evidence to suggest
that this regeneration process would have taken a violent form.
Violence, however, was implicit in this line of reasoning; for
Mariátegui believed that the *very act* of advancing the revolutionary cause elevated the participants morally and spiritually.
It therefore mattered little *when* the revolution occurred; participation was the primary activity required of the true revolutionary. Not only did Mariátegui believe that the struggle alone
was enough to reform and "redeem" men; but he also held that
culture was a primary instrument in reforming man and society. It is here that the role of the intellectual is of crucial
importance in Mariátegui's scheme of things. Through the
"conquest" of culture the forces of history could be righted in
Peru. The intellectuals could make a revolution without
violence—at least theoretically. The revolutionary, as Mariátegui often stated, was indeed a man of order, imbued with a
sense of history and its destiny.

This concern for the maintenance of order can be seen
throughout Mariátegui's writings. Indeed, the dominant
themes of racial and cultural pluralism and their resolution
through the establishment of a legitimate political order reflect

Mariátegui's main concern—to remove the political and personal uncertainty that characterized life in Peru for the mestizo and the intellectual. Mariátegui firmly believed that he was the "Spokesman"* for Peru's men-on-the-move—the "generation of 1919." This generation was caught in the uncertain social and psychological state that was caused by the social and economic change of the post-World War I era in Peru. They existed in the vacuum between tradition and modernity. This generation was, by virtue of education, foreign travel, and social position, a product of a modern world. The modernization process was slow to take place in Peru. The primordial requisites for "success" and achievement in Peruvian society were still denied to them; their personal aspirations did not fit an ascriptive society based on kinship, race, and family origins. Mariátegui and his generation wanted to shape their lives *and* society by their own individual actions, yet their society provided no outlet for these ambitions. The dispossessed of Mariátegui's generation were estranged from their society; and that estrangement was reflected in their commitment to revolution.

This estrangement best explains the concern of Mariátegui for completely transforming his society. Personal problems were projected onto the public level of politics since the political and social system was viewed as the primary cause of these personal problems. Mariátegui held that the political and social structure was illegitimate, primarily because he himself could find no place in it. Peru's social and political institutions were of alien origin, and the economy was also controlled by foreign interests; therefore Peru was still in a pre-national state. Political rights and obligations did not derive from civil society, but rather from pre-national social criteria—race, kinship, etc. Mariátegui wanted to change this condition by building a strong, unified state. The justification for this change was based

*See page 5.

on the *indigenista* ideas common in Peruvian literature, and vague Marxist principles.

The ideology of revolution then, was primarily an attempt to end Peru's pre-national condition. National integration would be accomplished by incorporating the Indian and his form of communal social organization into the fabric of this "new" Peru. The political order, once it was constituted upon this indigenous base, would be legitimate since it would rest upon the bulk of the population. Cultural pluralism would no longer be an obstacle to political and economic modernization. Once the gap of racial and cultural pluralism had been bridged, economic development would inevitably occur.

The creation of this new social and political order was to be led by the intellectuals, and Peru would be freed from its "alien exploiters." The founding of an economic order based on indigenous *and* Marxist principles would create a completely new Peru. Yet Mariátegui never fully developed this Marxist-indigenous synthesis; nor did he outline a detailed program for nation-building. He never made the transition from the realm of theory to that of political activism. This was in part due to his untimely death, yet Mariátegui's vision of a Peruvian national revolution has survived. Mariátegui is the towering figure in Peruvian political thought—the "Spokesman" of revolution.

Nowhere is this vision of Peruvian national revolution more apparent than in the rhetoric and programs of the military regime of General Juan Velasco Alvarado which seized power in October 1968. The regime has embarked on an avowedly nationalist program that closely parallels the program called for by Mariátegui. Yet the military regime at this writing possesses no coherent ideology. Indeed, if there is any ideological underpinning of the military government it is one of extreme nationalism. The military rulers are convinced that military government is, for the present, the only means of solving Peru's pressing problems. The military views itself as "developmentalist" and desirous of making a truly *Peruvian* "revolution" for Peru.[4] The military furthermore, believes that it is the only institution capable of avoiding the extremes of political and economic stagnation of the right, and a civil war on the left (similar to the pre-1959 Cuban situation that resulted in Castro's coming to power). It is then, a self-proclaimed balancer of the political system, controlling violent extremes while fostering gradual and controlled social change within the context of Peruvian cultural and political institutions.

This new sense of social consciousness has arisen particularly among the army officers; it is not so apparent among the air force and navy officers. The army has been in the vanguard of civic action programs, and of course has had to directly contend with the guerrilla uprising of La Convención in 1965 and 1966. In addition to civic action programs, the recruitment of army officers has been changing. More mestizos are being recruited, especially from the highlands. Indeed, the current president of Peru, General Juan Velasco Alvarado is from the town of Piura. He has never attended the military academy at Chorillos. Rather, he has risen through the ranks to reach his present position of General of Division. Velasco Alvarado's rise is indicative of the changing recruitment patterns in the Peruvian army; and these changing patterns in part account for the military's new social consciousness.

In addition to the above factors, the founding of the Centro de Altos Estudios Militares (Center for Advanced Military Studies) has fostered an increasing sense of social awareness. The center was organized in 1950 with the express mission of studying military-social problems. Staffed largely with civilian professors with decidedly leftist leanings, the Center has apparently succeeded in arousing the army officers to the need for social change in Peru. The Center still operates, and attendance is considered mandatory for any officer wishing to rise and gain major commands in the army.

While one cannot state categorically that the changing

recruitment and socialization patterns in the Peruvian army account for its recent behavior, the political attitudes and behavior of its officers are clearly different from naval and air force officers. Significantly, the present Peruvian military cabinet is composed almost entirely of army officers.[5]

Peru's new military leaders have gone further than any other regime in recent history in attempts to carry out basic reform programs. Some examples of the government's commitment to social reform are as follows:

> On October 3rd, 1968, the government expropriated the holdings of the International Petroleum Co. at Talara.[6]

> On September 3, 1969, the government decreed that United States mining firms had to make major capital investments or face nationalization.[7]

> Speaking on October 3, 1969, President Velasco Alvarado warned wealthy Peruvians who had investments abroad in banks and industry that the government expected them to reinvigorate the private sector of the Peruvian economy. Implicit in these remarks was the threat of expropriation of the estates held by these landholders, many of whom were absentee landlords.[8]

> The statement of October was followed on March 6, 1970, by the government's expropriation of the Chicama and Cartavio agricultural-industrial complexes. Significantly, Chicama, the largest single plantation complex in Peru comprising some 250,000 acres, was owned by wealthy Peruvians, not foreign landholders.[9]

These attempts at basic reform clearly indicate that the military has embarked on an extensive social restructuring of Peruvian society. However, like every nationalist reform-oriented group in Peru, the military regime has to contend with a major rival—APRA. Indeed, the success or failure of the military's reform program may hinge on its ability to develop a popular base of support independent of APRA. (Cooperation with

APRA has been unthinkable for the military since the APRA massacre of military personnel at Trujillo in 1932.) Evidence indicates that the military regime is attempting to forge a popular base. The Ministry of the Interior has launched a program of organization of workers into cooperatives loyal to the regime in an attempt to undercut APRA's traditional bases of mass support.

Clearly the military government is faced with a difficult task. It is intent upon freeing Peru from foreign economic exploitation at the expense of alienating some elements of the air force and navy officer corps. In addition it is committed to land reform as a basic means of incorporating the Indian into the social and political life of the country. The symbol of this reform is the portrait of Tupac Amaru which is now seen all over Peru. (Tupac Amaru was the Indian leader who organized the last resistance to Spanish colonial rule in 1780.) Clearly the military is seeking to steer a course mid-way between revolutionary violence of the left and stagnation of the right. Yet by vigorously pressing its reforms it may unleash the very forces of violence that it seeks to control. By becoming the institutional custodian of Peruvian nationalism the military has incorporated, and invokes most of the elements of Mariátegui's ideology. These have become so widely accepted in Peru that they may indeed induce the relative social quiescence necessary for the reforms to work.[10]

Mariátegui and his ideas still remain a vigorous force in Peruvian politics today. Yet the problems which he confronted still await their resolution. Peru still exists in a pre-national state. Fully two-thirds of the population lives outside the economic and political system. The problem of racial and cultural pluralism still exists; and this is especially painful to the educated mestizo. Social "success" is still based on race, kinship, and rank just as it was in Mariátegui's day. These "classic" political questions are the primary focus of reform politics in Peru. As long as they remain unresolved, Mariátegui will continue to exert a major influence on the political process. The revolution that he envisioned, whether peaceful or violent, will remain a distinct possibility, indeed, it may well be underway. However, in order to accomplish this "revolution," the military must co-opt the left-wing elements in Peru—especially the labor unions, intellectuals, and students. If this can be accomplished, the military, not the intellectuals, may indeed emerge as the true revolutionaries of modern Peru.

Appendix I

PROGRAM OF THE PERUVIAN SOCIALIST PARTY,

1928*

The program has to be a doctrinal declaration that affirms:

1. The international character of today's economy.
2. The international character of the revolutionary movement of the proletariat. The Socialist Party adapts its *praxis* to the concrete circumstances of the country; but it obeys a wide vision of class and the same national circumstances which are subordinated to the rhythm of world history. . . .
3. The contradictions of the capitalist economy grow sharper. [The shaky Peruvian economy of 1928, dependent on world markets, was beginning to experience severe dislocations.]
4. Capitalism finds itself in its imperialist stage. It is the capitalism of monopolies, of financial capital, of imperialist wars to capture markets and sources of raw materials. The *praxis* of Marxist socialism in this period is that of Marxism-Leninism. Marxism-Leninism is the revolutionary method of the stage of imperialism and monopolies. The Socialist Party of Peru, adopts it as its method of struggle.
5. . . . The emancipation of the economy of the country is possible only through the action of the proletarian masses, jointly bound with the world anti-imperialist struggle. Only proletarian action is able to stimulate first, and realize later, the tasks of the bourgeois revolution that the

*Ricardo Martínez de la Torre, *Apuntes para una interpretación marxista de la historia social del Perú*, 2nd ed., 4 vols. (Lima, 1947), vol. 2, pp. 398–402.

bourgeois Leguía regime is incompetent to develop and carry out.

6. Socialism finds the same idea in the substance of the indigenous communities . . . but this does not indicate in the absolute, a romantic and anti-historical tendency of reconstruction or recreation of Inca socialism, i.e., only the *habits* of cooperation and corporate life would be retained by the modern, "scientific" socialism.

7. Only socialism is able of resolving the problem of an education that is effectively democratic and equalitarian. . . . it is incompatible with the privileges of the capitalist order that condemns the poorer classes to cultural inferiority, and makes advanced education the monopoly of the rich.

8. Its bourgeois-democratic stage having been completed, the revolution becomes in its objectives and in its doctrine, a proletarian revolution. The party of the proletariat, empowered by the struggle for the exercise of power and the development of its own program, realizes in this stage the tasks of organization and defense of the socialist order.

9. The Socialist Party of Peru is the vanguard of the proletariat, the political force that assumes the task of direction and orientation in the struggle for the realization of its class ideals. . . .

. . . .

From the manifesto, the Party will direct a call to all of its followers, to the working masses, to work for the following immediate demands:

Full recognition of the freedom of association, assembly, and the workers' press

Recognition of the right of all workers to strike

Abolition of forced labor on road gangs

Establishment of social security and public assistance

Compliance with workers' accident laws and the protection of women and minors

Recognition of an eight-hour day in agricultural labor gangs

Establishment of a seven-hour day in the mines, and in other dangerous or unhealthy occupations

The obligation of mining and petroleum enterprises to recognize their workers . . . and all of the rights that the laws of the country guarantee them

Adjustment of the salaries of all workers in proportion to the cost of living, in accordance with the right of the workers for a better standard of living

Abolition of all forced, and gratuitous labor; and the abolition or punishment of the semi-slaveholding regimes in the highlands

Granting of latifundia lands to the indigenous communities for distribution among their members in proportion to their needs

Expropriation without indemnification, of all the funds of convents and religious congregations, in favor of the indigenous communities

Introduction of a salary and a minimum wage

Recognition of freedom of worship, and religious education, at least in terms of the articles of the Constitution, and consequently abolishing the last decree against non-Catholic schools

Public and free education in all grades

These are the principles for which the Socialist Party will struggle immediately. All of these correspond to the urgent exigencies of the material and intellectual emancipation of the masses. All of these have to be actively sustained by the proletariat, *and by the conscious elements of the middle class.* (italics added). The freedom of the Party to operate publicly and legally, the protection of the Constitution, and the guarantee that it accords to its citizens, in order to create and spread without restrictions its press, to carry out its meetings and debates, is a right demanded by the very act of the founding of this group. The tightly bound groups that today direct the people, resolutely assume by means of this manifesto, with responsibility and with the awareness of a historical duty, the mission of defending and propagating its principles and of maintaining and fostering its organization, at the cost of any sacrifice. . . .

Appendix II

CHRONOLOGY OF PRESIDENTS OF PERU

28 July, 1821	Peru declared independent of Spanish rule
1821–1822	José San Martín
1822–1823	José Antonio Sucre
1823–1826	Simón Bolívar
1826	General José de la Mar
1827	General Andrés Santa Cruz
1827–1829	Political anarchy—struggle among caudillos for the presidency
1829–1833	General Agustine Gámarra
1833–1836	Civil War (Three military factions vie for the presidency. The chief contenders were General Gámarra and General Salaverry)
1836–1839	General Andrés Santa Cruz (The period of the Confederacy of Peru and Bolivia)
1839–1844	Civil War (An eight-sided caudillo struggle for presidency)

1845–1851	General Ramón Castilla
1851–1855	General José Rufino Echineque
1855–1862	General Ramón Castilla
1862–1865	General Juan Antonio Pezet
1865–1868	General Pedro Diéz Canseco
1868–1872	Colonel José Balta
1872–1876	Manuel Pardo
1876–1879	Mariano Ignacio Prado
1879–1881	No effective Peruvian government as Prado departed for Europe ostensibly to secure funds for the conduct of the War of the Pacific.
1881–1884	Chilean military occupation of Lima
1885–1890	General Andrés Cáceres
1890–1895	Colonel Remegio Morales Bermúdez
1895–1899	Nicolás de Piérola
1899–1903	Eduardo de Romaña
May, 1903–May, 1904	Miguel Candamo
May, 1904–Sept, 1904	Serapio Calderón
Sept, 1904–Sept, 1908	José Pardo y Barreja
1908–1912	Augusto B. Leguía
1912–Feb, 1914	Guillermo Billinghurst
Feb, 1914–Aug, 1915	Colonel Oscar R. Benavides (acting president)
Sept, 1915–Sept, 1919	José Pardo
1919–1930	Augusto B. Leguía
1930–1933	Colonel Luis M. Sánchez Cerro
1933–1939	General Oscar R. Benavides
1939–1945	Manuel Prado Ugarteche
1945–1948	José Bustamente y Rivero
1948–1956	General Manuel Odría
1956–1962	Manuel Prado Ugarteche
July, 1962–July, 1963	Military junta rules
July, 1963–Oct, 1968	Fernando Belaúnde Terry
Oct, 1968–present	General Juan Velasco Alvarado

Appendix III

THE PERUVIAN POLITICAL SYSTEM:

A SUMMARY

The Constitution of 1933 is the one currently in force in Peru. It is the eleventh of a series dating back to 1823. However, the provisions of the 1933 Constitution have been amended from time to time. In 1939 the president, General Oscar Benavides, wished to strengthen the presidential powers. Following a plebiscite, the Benavides reforms were adopted, only to be annulled by the APRA controlled Congress of 1945. To date, this Constitution is still in force though the ruling junta has publicly stated that it will attempt to draw up a new constitution before surrendering power.

The President:

Perhaps the most important section of the Constitution deals with the powers of the chief executive. While sovereignty rests with the nation, the president is declared to be the "personification" of the nation (Article 134). He not only represents the nation at home and abroad, but is also *personally* responsible for maintaining internal security. He is empowered to convene Congress, nominate and dismiss the president of the Council of Ministers and all other ministers of state. Furthermore, the president can dictate decrees, administer the national income, direct diplomatic negotiations, and appoint and dismiss ambassadors. His term is six years, and he may not serve a successive term.

The Military:

In the light of the recent military coup of October 1969, it is also worth noting the constitutional provisions which govern the position of the military in the political process. The 1933 Constitution states that the purpose of the armed forces is to assure the rights of the nation, compliance with the Constitution, and preserve public order (Article 213). While the president is charged with maintaining internal security and is authorized to use the military in this function (Article 154), he may *not* take direct command of the military and remain president (Article 145). He is not, therefore, the commander-in-chief while president.

The president's principal advisers on military matters are the three co-equal and independent service ministers. These are usually active members of the respective military services— army, air, and navy. Directly subordinate, and immediately responsible to each minister is the commander-in-chief of each service. In addition, the president is advised on military matters by three other organs; the Supreme Council of National Defense, the Joint Command of the Armed Forces, and the National Intelligence Service. The Supreme Council of National Defense is composed of the president of the Council of Ministers, the three service representatives, the Minister of Government and Police, the Minister of Foreign Affairs, the Minister of Finance and Commerce, and the president of the Joint Command of the Armed Forces. This Supreme Council is similar in structure and purpose to the National Security Council in the United States. (The Joint Command was established by presidential decree in 1957.)

Article 214 of the Constitution requires every Peruvian to contribute toward national defense, and to submit to military obligations. The legislation based on this statute provides for selective service based on a lottery system for all males between the ages of 18 and 25 for a period of two years service. Those failing to register are immediately inducted.

The Legislature:

Legislation is enacted by a bi-cameral Congress comprising the Senate and the Chamber of Deputies. The Senate numbers 40, the Chamber 140. The term of office is six years which coincides with the presidential term. However, members of Congress may run for immediate re-election. Under the Constitution, the Congress also sits as an electoral body to select a president if no candidate has received one-third of the popular vote in a regular election.

The 1945 amendments to the Constitution attempted to curb the power of the president. As a result of these amendments, the president was required to obtain the confirmation of Congress for all nominees to ministerial posts. He also lost his power of veto. The chief minister, the president of the Council of Ministers, was required to outline his policy proposals to Congress, and Congress was given the power to censure ministers. Yet, while Congress can oust a minister it cannot appoint one. Control of the Council of Ministers still effectively lies with the president.

The Judiciary:

The Judiciary consists of a Supreme Court which convenes in Lima. There are also lower courts which convene in the departments and provinces. Members of the Supreme Court are chosen by Congress from a list of ten nominees submitted by the president. The president also nominates candidates for judicial positions on the lower courts. The political influence of the president therefore, is paramount in the judicial system just as in the other branches of the national government.

Administration of justice is extremely slow despite the large number of practicing lawyers; and the time spent in jail awaiting trial is often longer than the sentence that is awarded once a case is heard.

The Church:

The 1933 Constitution officially recognized the Roman Catholic Church as the "official" Church (Article 232). While religious freedom is guaranteed, instruction in the Catholic faith is compulsory in the public schools. The Constitution provides that relations with the Church be defined by a concordat, though none has ever been signed with the Vatican. The Church continues to receive financial support from the Peruvian treasury, though the amount is not public knowledge. The president of the republic retains the right to present candidates to the Vatican for the major Church offices in Peru. All candidates are required by the Constitution to be native-born Peruvian nationals.

Local Administration:

Peru is divided into twenty-three departments and the province of Callao. Departments are sub-divided into districts and provinces. As in the French system, the chief administrative officer is the prefect. Sub-prefects and governors administer smaller areas. Lieutenant-governors are appointed as necessary. Appointments to prefecture are made by the president. Governors are appointed by the prefect, and lieutenant-governors by the sub-prefect. During the Belaúnde regime, elections were held which were designed to grant greater local autonomy to the departments and provinces. It remains to be seen whether the central government will continue to be willing to divest itself of administrative control of these local units. Under the present military regime, such a diminution of central control of the provinces seems highly unlikely.

The Electoral Process:

Under present rules, political parties must register with the Jurado Nacional de Elecciones (The Electoral Court) and present a list of sixty-thousand members to nominate a presidential Candidate and twenty-thousand members to nominate candidates for the Congress. A nominee must meet all legal requirements for office. In addition, he must file signatures of petition in support of his candidacy and a fee varying from 30,000 soles for presidential candidates to 2000 soles for senatorial candidates, and 1000 soles for candidates to the Chamber of Deputies.

All literate Peruvian nationals, both males and females, under the age of sixty are required to register and vote. However, this regulation is seldom strictly enforced. The literacy requirement effectively eliminates the bulk of the population, the Indians, from the electoral process. In national elections, the balance of power resides in the urban areas, especially Lima.

The voting act is governed strictly. Polls are open from eight a.m. until four p.m. All campaigning ceases forty-eight hours prior to election day, and sale of alcholic beverages is prohibited on election day. Candidates for office, electoral officials, and party officials cannot be arrested unless they commit a serious crime. The government supplies the ballots and the Electoral Court counts the results.

It must be noted however that electoral results have often been nullified in the past by the military. Most recently this occurred in 1962, when the military intervened and declared the election void. The coup of October 1968 has been viewed by many observers as a military move to nullify the results of the approaching 1969 presidential elections when projections had given APRA the victory.

Notes

CHAPTER 1—Notes

[1] For a discussion of this distinction see: Kalman H. Silvert, *The Conflict Society: Reaction and Revolution in Latin America,* (New York: 1966), pp. 18–22.

See also: John M. Baines, "José Mariátegui and the Ideology of Revolution in Peru," *Rocky Mountain Social Science Journal.* Vol. 7, No. 2. (October, 1970) pp. 109–116. (The editor's permission to use this material is gratefully acknowledged.)

[2] Cf. Genaro García Checa, *La acción escrita: José Carlos Mariátegui periodista* (Lima: Imprenta Torres Aguirre, 1964); V. Miroshevsky, "El populismo en el Perú: papel de Mariátegui en la historia del pensamiento latino-americano," *Dialéctica,* Vol. 1, No. 1 (Havana: May-June, 1942), pp. 41–49: Jorge del Prado, "Mariátegui, Marxista-Leninista," *Democrácia y trabajo,* No. 88 (Lima: December 1, 1943): S. Simionov and A. Shulgovsky, "El papel de José Carlos Mariátegui en la formación del Partido Comunista del Perú," *Hora del hombre,* Vol. 1, No. 1 (Lima: Jan., 1960)

[3] Manuel González Prada, *Páginas libres* 1st ed. (Lima: 1894).
————. *Horas de lucha* (Callao, Peru: 1924)
————. *Anarquía* (Santiago de Chile: 1940)

[4] The idea of racial and cultural pluralism and its relationship to national integration has been suggested by Clifford Geertz. See: "The Integrative Revolution: Primordial Sentiments and Civil Politics in the New States," in Geertz, ed. *Old Societies and New States* (New York: 1963), pp. 112–113. The Geertz classifications are, assumed racial and blood ties, language, region, and custom.

[5] These goals are stated in Mariátegui's best known work. See: José Carlos Mariátegui, *Siete ensayos de interpretación de la realidad peruna,* 8th ed. (Lima: 1963)

[6] Daniel J. Lerner, *The Passing of Traditional Society* (New York: 1958)

[7] Ibid., p. 407.

[8] Mariátegui, "La tradición nacional," *Mundial* 7. No. 390. (Lima: Dec. 2, 1927)

————. "El factor religioso," *Mundial* 7. No. 391. (Lima: Dec. 9, 1927)

[9] These elements form the fundamental themes of Mariátegui's *Siete ensayos.*

[10] The goals of the military regime are stated in an interview with General Velasco Alvarado entitled: "Perú por fin es libre," *Life en español* Vol. 34, No. 1 (México, D.F.: July 14, 1969) pp. 14–17.

CHAPTER 2—Notes

[1] This thesis is most cogently defended by Jorge Basadre in his definitive history of Peru. See: Jorge Basadre, *Historia de la República del Perú,* 3rd ed., 2 vols. (Lima: 1946) See Appendix II for a chronology of presidents of Peru.

[2] César Antonio Ugarte, "La política agraria de la república," *Mercurio Peruano,* Vol. 6, No. 59 (Lima: May, 1923)

[3] Two sources which manage to capture some of the intense feeling generated by the war and its aftermath are: Graham H. Stuart, *The Tacna-Arica Dispute* (Boston: 1927), and W. J. Dennis, *Tacna and Arica* (New Haven, Conn.: 1931).

[4] For a good survey of González Prada's works and his era see: W. Rex Crawford, *A Century of Latin American Thought* (2nd ed.; Cambridge, Mass.: 1961), pp. 173–182. Robert E. McNichol, "Intellectual Origins of Aprismo," *Hispanic American Historical Review,* Vol. 23, No. 3 (August, 1943), pp. 424–40. Hereafter cited as McNichol.

[5] Cf. Harold E. Davis, *Latin American Social Thought* (Washington, D.C.: 1961), pp. 190–96 and McNichol. pp. 424–40.

[6] Manuel González Prada, "El artista y el obrero," *Horas de lucha* (Callao, Peru: 1924), pp. 63–77.

[7] González Prada, "Nuestros indios," *Horas de lucha* (Callao, Peru: 1924), pp. 311–38.

[8] Ibid., p. 311.

[9] Ibid., pp. 311–38.

[10] This complex period will be taken up in detail in the next chapter. A good survey article is: Luis Alberto Sánchez, "Mariátegui y Valdelomar," *Mundial,* Vol. 10, No. 514 (Lima: April 26, 1930).

[11]José Carlos Mariátegui, "González Prada," *Amauta,* Vol. 2, No. 16 (Lima: July, 1928), pp. 8–15.

CHAPTER 3—Notes

[1]Guillermo Rouillón, a noted Peruvian Mariátegui scholar, states that Mariátegui was not born in Lima, but in the town of Moquegua far to the south. He holds that Mariátegui, according to baptismal records, was born on July 16, 1894. All other biographers list the date as July 14, 1895, and the birthplace as Lima. Since I did not see the records in Moquegua, I have used the more commonly accepted date and place of birth.

[2]Eugenio Chang-Rodríquez, *La literatura política de González Prada, Mariátegui y Haya de la Torre* (Mexico: 1957), p. 130. It should be noted here that Mariategui's father was white, and his mother a mestiza (of white and Indian ancestry). Rouillón contends that records in Callao show the date of death of Mariátegui's father as 1907. Mariátegui's mother died in Lima in 1948.

[3]This aspect of Mariátegui's personality was mentioned by Guillermo Rouillón and Eudocio Ravines in interviews (see bibliography for dates).

[4]For Mariátegui's comments on the educational system as it related to the structure of Peruvian society see: José Carlos Mariátegui, *La reforma universitaria* (Buenos Aires: 1928). This slim volume is a reprint of articles appearing in *Amauta,* Nos. 12 and 13.

[5]The pseudonyms used by Mariátegui were: Juan Croniquer, J. C., Jack, Monsieur Camomille, Sigfrid, El Cronista Criollo, El de Siempre, and X. Y. Z.

[6]*Colónida,* Nos. 1–4 (Lima: Jan. 15, 1916 to May 1, 1916). Abraham Valdelomar, *Obras escogidas* (Lima: 1947). The introductory essay entitled, "Colónida y Valdelomar," was written by Mariátegui. It is an excellent description of the *Colónida* movement. Luis Alberto Sánchez, "Mariátegui y Valdelomar," *Mundial,* Vol. 10, No. 514 (Lima: April 26, 1930).

[7]Ibid. This is my hypothesis, which I have based on the available sources, especially Mariátegui's essay in the Valdelomar collection.

[8]For an idea of Mariátegui's deep torment see: José Carlos Mariátegui, "Plegaria del cansancio," "Coloquio sentimental," and "Insomnio," *Colónida,* No. 3 (Lima: March 1, 1916), pp. 26–27.

NOTES 161

⁹Mariátegui always had to live by his pen and many of his articles had little or nothing to do with his political views. They were written to provide an income. From about 1925 on, he wrote an average of two to three articles per week.

¹⁰See: Juan Croniquer [Mariátegui], "Afirmación. Fantasia lunática," *El Tiempo* (Lima: July 28, 1916), p. 8. "Elogio de la celda ascética," *El Tiempo* (Lima: August 28, 1916), p. 3.

¹¹This renunciation appeared in a letter to the editor of *Nuestra Época*. See: *Nuestra Época* (Lima: June 22, 1918).

¹²For a more detailed explanation of this projection of Mariátegui's personal conflict upon public affairs see a concept developed in: Harold D. Lasswell, *Psychopathology and Politics* (New York: 1930).

¹³For some striking statistics relating to this imbalance in the Peruvian economy see: Ricardo Martínez de la Torre, *Apuntes para una interpretación marxista de la historia social del Perú,* 2d ed., 4 Vols. (Lima: 1947–49), Vol. 1, p. 16.

¹⁴For Mariátegui's comments on the Futurists and his subsequent break with them see: "El joven Perú," *El Tiempo* (Lima: September 20, 1918), p. 2. "Partidos militantes," *El Tiempo* (Lima: September 26, 1918), p. 1. "Papeles, papeles, papeles," *El Tiempo* (Lima: October 26, 1918), p. 1.

¹⁵Cf. Mariátegui, "La voz de Leguía," *El Tiempo* (Lima, Peru: May 2, 1917), p. 1. "Leguía viene," *El Tiempo* (Lima: March 6, 1918), p. 1. "Nuestros Carlistas," *El Tiempo* (Lima: July 20, 1918), p. 2. "Voto sensacional," *El Tiempo* (Lima: October 8, 1918), p. 2.

¹⁶Mariátegui writes of his break with the Futurists and the progress of his "ideological definition" in the prologue to the first of a three article series by Martínez de la Torre. See: Ricardo Martínez de la Torre, "El movimiento obrero en 1919," *Amauta,* No. 17 (Lima: September, 1928).

¹⁷Mariátegui, *La reforma universitaria* (Buenos Aires: 1928). This is a reprint of articles that appeared in numbers 12 and 13 of *Amauta.* For detailed information on the University Reform Movement, see the definitive work: Gabriel del Mazo, *La reforma universitaria,* 3 vols. (Buenos Aires: 1928).

¹⁸Cf. Harry Kantor, *The Ideology and Program of the Peruvian Aprista Party* (Berkeley, Cal.: 1953). Robert E. McNichol, "The Intellectual Origins of Aprismo," *Hispanic American Historical Review,* Vol. 23, No. 3 (August, 1943), pp. 424–40. Luis Alberto Sánchez, *Haya de la Torre o el político* (Santiago de Chile: 1936).

[19]For a different treatment of the Leguía regime see: Frederick B. Pike, *The Modern History of Peru,* 2nd ed. (New York: 1969), pp. 217–49.

[20]The 1940 census classified 41,945 or 0.68 per cent of the population as "yellow" race. See: R. J. Owens, *Peru* (London: 1963), p. 11.

[21]Following his return from Europe, Mariátegui tried to lay to rest the charge that he had "sold out" to Leguía. To this charge was added the argument that he was an Europeanized intellectual who no longer understood Peru. This will be taken up at length in discussing Mariátegui's later career.

CHAPTER 4—Notes

[1]José Carlos Mariátegui, *Defensa del Marxismo,* 2nd ed. (Lima: 1964), p. 129.

[2]For a good survey see: Peter H. Gay, *The Dilemma of Democratic Socialism* (New York: 1962). The French socialist movement is described brilliantly in Chapter 8 of Barbara W. Tuchman, *The Proud Tower* (New York: 1966).

[3]This inscription on the tomb of Mariátegui is a passage from a eulogy written by Barbusse. It was last published on the twenty-fifth anniversary of the death of Mariátegui. See: *La Crónica* (Lima: April 15, 1955), p. 14.

[4]Henrí Barbusse, *We Others,* translated by Fitzwater Wray (New York: 1918).

[5]Barbusse, *The Inferno,* translated by Edward J. O'Brien (New York: 1918).

[6]Barbusse, *Jesus,* translated by Salon Librescot (New York: 1927). For Mariátegui's review of this work see: José Carlos Mariátegui, "Jesus' de Henrí Barbusse," *Variedades* (Lima: June 25, 1927).

[7]George L. Mosse, *The Culture of Western Europe* (New York: 1961), p. 184.

[8]Barbusse, *Clarté* (Paris: 1919).

[9]Barbusse, *Le Couteau entre les Dents* (Paris: 1921).

[10]Ibid., pp. 50–52.

[11]Ibid., p. 7.

[12]Ibid.

[13]Mariátegui, *La escena contemporánea* (Lima: 1959), p. 94.

> El ideal de nuestra época. . . . El órden nuevo, el órden revolucionario, racionalizará y humanizará las costumbres. Resolverá los problemas que, a causa de su estructura y de su función, el orden burgués es impotente para solucionar. Consentirá la liberación de la mujer de la servidumbre doméstica, asegurará la educación social de los niños, libertará al matrimonio de las preocupaciones económicas. El socialismo . . . acusado de materialista, resulta, en suma, desde este punto de vista, una reivindicación, un renacimiento de valores espirituales y morales, oprimidos por la organización y los métodos capitalistas. Sí en la época capitalista prevalecieron ambiciones e intereses materiales, la época proletaria, sus modalidades y sus instituciones se inspirarán en intereses e ideales éticos.

[14]Ibid., p. 11.

[15]The three works cited below were probably the most influential on Mariátegui: Miguel de Unamuno y Jugo, *La Vida de Don Quijote y Sancho* (Madrid: 1961), *Del sentimiento trágico de la vida* (Madrid: 1912), *The Agony of Christianity,* translated by Ernest Boyd (New York: 1928).

[16]Mariátegui, *El alma matinal* (Lima: 1959), p. 21.

[17]Mariátegui, *Signos y obras* (Lima: 1959), pp. 116–20.

[18]Mariátegui, *La escena contemporánea* (Lima: 1959), pp. 13–41 and pp. 136–42.

[19]Ibid., pp. 14, 16–17.

[20]Ibid., p. 16.

> Mussolini no dió un espiritu, un programa, al fascismo. Al contrario, el fascismo dió su espiritu á Mussolini. . . . Mussolini necesitó asimilar, absorber el antisocialismo, el chauvinismo de la clase media para encuadrar y organizar a ésta en las filas de los *fasci di combatimento.*

[21]Ibid., pp. 13–18.

[22]Ibid., pp. 13–41.

[23]Mariátegui expressed his love for Anna in a verse entitled, "La vida que tu me díste." It is reproduced in : Maria Wiesse, *José Carlos Mariátegui* (Lima: 1945), p. 43.

[24]Guillermo Rouillón stated that Mariátegui never knew Croce intimately, that he met him briefly at the Chiappe pension. Whatever their personal relationship, Mariátegui was familiar with Croce's works.

[25]Mariátegui, "Gorki, Rusia y Cristóbal Castro," *Mundial,* Vol. 8, No. 425 (Lima: Aug. 3, 1928).

[26]Mariátegui, *La escena contemporánea,* pp. 142–46.

[27]Ibid., p. 14 and, "Algo sobre el fascismo," *El Tiempo* (Lima: June 29, 1921), p. 3.

[28]Mariátegui, *La escena contemporánea,* p. 50. *Siete ensayos . . .* pp. 9–89.

[29]Mariátegui, *Siete ensayos* pp. 9–89.

[30]Mariátegui, *El alma matinal* (Lima: 1959), p. 21.

[31]Ibid., p. 21

[32]Ibid., p. 22.

CHAPTER 5—Notes

[1]This idea of "consecration" was not a new one in Latin America. It had occurred most notably in Mexico and Ecuador in the nineteenth century. It was often a means whereby the existing regime gained the powerful support of the Church. For the Church, it served to eliminate all other forms of religious worship. Placing a nation under the protection of the Sacred Heart of Jesus was no guarantee of peace and stability. Divine protection was not forthcoming in Mexico during the *Reforma,* nor in Ecuador during and after the García-Moreno dictatorship. The move by Leguía in Peru can be most logically viewed as a means of shoring up the president's shaky support among the clerical and land-holding interests.

[2]For similar accounts of this encounter see: Eugenio Chang-Rodríquez, *La literatura política . . .,* p. 141. Armando Bazán, *Biografía de José Carlos Mariátegui* (Lima: 1939), p. 99.

[3]Mariátegui, "Una encuesta á José Carlos Mariátegui," *Mundial,* Vol. 7, No. 319 (Lima: July 23, 1926).

[4]Mariátegui, *Historia de la crisis mundial* (Lima, Peru: 1959), pp. 15–25. This is a collection of speeches given at the Popular Universities. Hereafter cited as *Historia.*

[5]Jorge del Prado, *Mariátegui y su obra* (Lima: 1946), p. 21. See also: *Claridad,* Vol. 5, No. 5 (Lima: September, 1923). Note: The numbering and dates of *Claridad* are irregular. Pagination is either irregular, or non-existent.

[6]*Historia,* pp. 15–25.

[7]Mariátegui, "Presentación," *Claridad,* I, No. 1 (Lima: May, 1923).

[8]Mariátegui, "El asunto de Claridad," *La Crónica,* Vol. 12, No. 4523 (Lima: January 15, 1924).

[9]*Historia.* In later years Haya de la Torre claimed that these lectures had been edited, and did not accurately state Mariátegui's position in 1923–1924. See: Argos [pseudonym for Haya de la Torre], "Bio-bibliografía de José Carlos Mariátegui," *La Tribuna,* Vol. 7 (Lima: January 26, 1964), p. 6.

[10]Mariátegui, "¡ Trabajadores manuales e intelectuales !," *El obrero textile,* Vol. 5, No. 59 (Lima: May 1, 1924), p. 3.

[11]All of Mariátegui's biographers relate this basic account.

[12]Mariátegui, "Palabras de Mariátegui," *Claridad,* Vol. 2, No. 6 (Lima: September, 1924), p. 3.

[13]Haya's political personality can perhaps best be placed in perspective by repeating an anecdote told me by Eudocio Ravines in Lima (Sept. 14, 1966). Ravines, who was an early associate of Haya, tells of the time in 1927 when he and Haya were members of the Peruvian delegation to the Anti-Imperialist Congress in Brussels. Haya's good friend José Vasconcelos headed the Mexican delegation. One day, while at lunch, Vasconcelos began chiding Haya about the lack of ideology and the personalism of the APRA movement. Haya, usually a teetotaler, had drunk some wine at his friend's insistence and had become somewhat flushed. Vasconcelos kept up his banter throughout the meal. Finally Haya got up and left while the others were paying the check. Vasconcelos then called out, "You my friend without a program, wait for us!" Livid, Haya turned shouting, "I don't need a program. The most important thing is power, power, and *power.*"

[14]Mariátegui, "El ocaso de la civilización europea," *Claridad,* Vol. 1, No. 1 (Lima: May 1, 1923), pp. 16–18.

[15]Ibid. pp. 16–18.

[16]*Historia,* pp. 15–25, 106–118.

[17]*Historia,* pp. 33–40.

[18]*Historia,* pp. 134–39.

[19]Cf. Mariátegui, "Hacia el estudio de los problemas peruanos," *Mundial,* Vol. 6, No. 265 (Lima: July 10, 1925). "Nacionalismo realista," *Mundial,* Vol. 6, No. 266 (Lima: July 17, 1925). "El Indio de la República," *Mundial,* Vol. 6, No. 276 (Lima: September 25, 1925).

[20]Cf. Mariátegui, "Pasadismo y futurismo," *Mundial,* Vol. 5, No. 229 (Lima: October 31, 1924). "El rostro y el alma del Twantinsuyo," *Mundial,* Vol. 6, No. 274 (Lima: September 11, 1925).

[21]Mariátegui, "La urbe y el campo," *Mundial,* Vol. 5, No. 229 (Lima: Oct. 3, 1924).

[22]Mariátegui, "La unidad de la América Indo-Española," *Variedades* (Lima: Dec. 6, 1924).

[23]Mariátegui, "La crisis universitaria," *Claridad,* Vol. 1, No. 2 (Lima: n.d.).

[24]This is a summary of the *Mundial* article cited in note 20.

[25]It should be noted that Mariátegui's idealization of the indigenous elements in Peru's history paralleled those of Haya de la Torre. Doubtless both men were familiar with the writings of Mexico's José Vasconcelos, and it seems quite likely that these writings influenced both Mariátegui's concept of *indigenismo* and Haya de la Torre's concept of Indo-América. See: José Vasconcelos, *La raza cósmica: misión de la raza iberoamericana* (Paris: n.d.); Mariátegui, "Indología por José Vasconcelos," *Variedades,* Vol. 23, No. 1025 (Lima: Oct. 22, 1927). For other interpretations of the Inca heritage, see: Louis Bauden, *L'Empire Socialiste des Inca* (Paris: 1928) Garcilaso de la Vega el Inca, *Comentarios reales de los Incas,* 2 vols. (Buenos Aires: 1943).

[26]Mariátegui, "Nacionalismo y vanguardismo," *Mundial,* Vol. 6, No. 285 (Lima: Nov. 27, 1925). "Nacionalismo y vanguardismo en la literatura y en el arte," *Mundial,* Vol. 6, No. 286 (Lima: December 4, 1925). "Nacionalismo e internacionalismo," *Mundial,* Vol. 5, No. 230 (Lima: October 10, 1924).

[27]Mariátegui, "El progreso nacional y el capital humano," *Mundial,* Vol. 6, No. 278 (Lima: October 9, 1925).

[28]Mariátegui, "La institución de la República," *Mundial,* Vol. 7, No. 241 (Lima: Dec. 24, 1926).

[29]Mariátegui, "Nacionalismo y vanguardismo . . .,"

[30]Ibid.

[31]Mariátegui, "Economía colonial," *Mundial,* Vol. 7, No. 291 (Lima: January 8, 1926). "Aspectos del problema indígena," *Mundial,* Vol. 7, No. 340 (Lima: December 17, 1926).

CHAPTER 6—Notes

[1] José Carlos Mariátegui, "Presentación de 'Amauta'," *Amauta,* Vol. 1, No. 1 (Lima: September, 1926), p. 3. Hereafter cited as "Presentacion."

[2] Mariátegui, "¿Cómo escribe usted?" *Variedades,* Vol. 22, No. 932 (Lima: January 9, 1926), pp. 11-12.

[3] Genaro García Checa, *La acción escrita* (Lima: 1964), p. 190. The figure given by Checa seems about right. I have approximated the value in $ U.S. using the exchange rate of the middle 1920's of 5 soles to the U.S. dollar.

[4] "Presentación,"

Esta revista, en el campo intelectual, no representa un grupo. Representa, mas bien, un movimiento un espíritu. En el Perú se siente desde hace algún tiempo una corriente, cada día mas vigorosa y definida, de renovación. A los fautores de esta renovación se les llama vanguardistas, socialistas, revolucionarios etc. La historia no los ha bautizado definitivamente todavía. Existen entre ellos algunas discrepancias formales, algunas diferencias psicológicas. Pero por encima de lo que los diferencia, todos estos espíritus ponen lo que los aproxima y mancomuna: su voluntad de crear un Perú nuevo dentro del mundo nuevo. La inteligencia, la coordinación de los mas volitivos de estos elementos, progresan gradualmente. El movimiento—intelectual y espiritual—adquiere poco a poco organicidad. Con la aparición de "AMAUTA" entra en una fase de definición.

"AMAUTA" ha tenido un proceso normal de gestación. No nace de súbito por determinación exclusivamente mía. Yo vine de Europa con el propósito de fundar una revista. Dolorosas vicisitudes personales no me permitieron cumplirlo. Pero este tiempo no ha transcurrido en balde. Mi esfuerzo se ha articulado con el de otros intelectuales y artistas que piensan y sienten parecidamente a mí. Hace dos años, esta revista habría sido una voz un tanto personal. Ahora es la voz de un movimiento y de una generación.

El primer resultado que los escritores de "AMAUTA" nos proponemos obtener es el de acordarnos y conocernos mejor nosotros mismos. *El trabajo de la revista nos solidarizará más.* Al mismo tiempo que atraerá á ostros buenos elementos, alejará á algunos fluctuantes y desganados que por ahora coquetean con el vanguardismo, pero que apenas éste les demande un sacrificio, se apresuraran a dejarlo. "AMAUTA" *cribará a los hombres de la vanguardia—militantes y simpatizantes—hasta separar la paja del grano. Producirá o precipitará un fenómeno de polarización y concentración.*

No hace falta declarar expresamente que "AMAUTA" no es una tribuna libre abierta a todos los vientos del espíritu. *Los que fundamos esta revista no concebimos una cultura y un arte agnósticos.* Nos sentimos una fuerza beligerante, polémica. No le hacemos ninguna concesión al criterio generalmente faláz de la tolerancia de las ideas. Para nosotros hay ideas buenas e ideas malas. En el prólogo de mi libro "La Escena Contemporánea" escribí que soy un hombre con una filiación y una fé. Lo mismo puedo decir de esta revista, que rechaza todo lo que es contrario a su ideología así como todo lo que no traduce ideología alguna.

Para presentar "Amauta", están demas las palabras solemnes. Quiero proscribir de esta revista la retórica. Me parecen absolutamente inútiles los programas. El Perú es un páis de rótulos y de etiquetas. Hagamos al fin alguna cosa con contenido, vale decir con espíritu. "Amauta" por otra parte no tiene necesidad de un programa; tiene necesidad tan solo de un destino, de un objeto.

El titulo preocupará probablemente a algunos. Esto se deberá a la importancia excesiva, fundamental, que tiene entre nosotros el rótulo. No se mire en este caso a la acepción estricta de la palabra. *El titulo no traduce sino nuestra adhesión a la Raza, no refleja sino nuestro homenaje al Incaismo. Pero especificamente la palabra "Amauta" adquiere con esta revista una nueva acepción. La vamos a crear otra vez.*

El objeto de esta revista es el de plantear, esclarecer y conocer los problemas peruanos desde puntos de vista doctrinarios y científicos. Pero consideraremos siempre al Perú dentro del panorama del mundo. Estudiaremos todos los grandes movimientos de renovación-políticos, filosóficos, artísticos, literarios, científicos. Todo lo humano es nuestro. Esta revista vinculará a los hombres nuevos del Perú, primero con los de los otros pueblos de América, en seguida con los de los otros pueblos del mundo.

Nada más agregaré. Habrá que ser muy poco perspicaz para no darse cuenta de que al Perú le nace en este momento una revista histórica. [italics added]

[5] Another approach in analyzing *Amauta* is presented in: Alberto Tauro, *Amauta y su influencia* (Lima: 1926), pp. 7-12.

[6] Cf. Luis Valcárcel, "Tempestad en los Andes," *Amauta,* Vol. 1, No. 1 (Lima: September, 1926), pp. 4-6. Victor Raúl Haya de la Torre, "Romain Rolland y la América Latina," *Amauta,* Vol. 1, No. 2 (Lima: October, 1926), pp. 12-13. José Carlos Mariátegui, "La evolución de la economía peruana," *Amauta,* Vol. 1, No. 2 (Lima: October, 1926), pp. 29-32.

[7] Mariátegui, "Nota polémica," *Amauta,* Vol. 2, No. 6 (Lima: February, 1927), p. 29.

[8] Mariátegui, "Arte, revolución, y decadencia," *Amauta,* Vol. 1, No. 3 (Lima: November, 1926), pp. 3-4.

[9] Mariátegui, "Mensaje al Congreso Obrero," *Amauta,* Vol. 2, No. 5 (Lima: January, 1927), pp. 35-36.

[10] Luis Alberto Sánchez, "Batiburillo indigenista," *Mundial,* Vol. 2, No. 349 (Lima: Feb. 18, 1927). "Respuesta á José Carlos Mariátegui," *Mundial,* Vol. 7, No. 351 (Lima: March 4, 1927). "Ismos contra ismos," *Mundial,* Vol. 7, No. 352 (Lima: March 11, 1927).

[11] Mariátegui, "Polémica finita," *Amauta,* Vol. 2, No. 7 (Lima: March, 1927), pp. 6, 23. "Indigenismo y socialismo: intermezzo polémico," *Amauta,* Vol. 2, No. 7 (Lima: March, 1927), pp. 37–39. Hereafter cited "Intermezzo."

[12] "Intermezzo."

[13] Ibid.

[14] Ibid.

[15] Mariátegui, "La reacción en México," *Variedades,* Vol. 22, No. 962 (Lima: August 7, 1926). "La guerra civil en México." *Variedades,* Vol. 23, No. 1024 (Lima: Oct. 15, 1927).

[16] For the shift in Mariátegui's view of the Chinese Revolution cf: Mariátegui, "Las nuevas jornadas de la Revolución China," *Variedades,* Vol. 22, No. 947 (Lima: April 24, 1926). "Lo que el cable no dice," *Mundial,* Vol. 9, No. 487 (Lima: October 18, 1929).

[17] Mariátegui, "Después de la muerte de Dzerjinsky," *Variedades,* Vol. 22, No. 964 (Lima: August 21, 1926).

[18] An exchange of letters between Haya de la Torre and Mariátegui is reproduced in the following: Luis Alberto Sánchez, *Haya de la Torre o el político* (Santiago de Chile: 1936), p. 141. Hereafter cited as *Político.* Ricardo Martínez de la Torre, *Apuntes para una interpretación marxista de la historia social del Perú,* Vol. 2, pp. 213–375. (This is the most detailed treatment I could find, though the author is a supporter of Mariátegui.)

[19] *Político,* p. 141.

[20] Mariátegui, "Sobre el fraguado complot comunista," *La Crónica,* Vol. 14, No. 7072 (Lima: June 12, 1927), p. 15.

[21] Ibid. p. 15.

[22] Mariátegui, "Segundo acto," *Amauta,* Vol. 2, No. 10 (Lima: December, 1927), p. 3.

Todos los lectores de "Amauta" están enterados de las razones por las cuales nuestra revista ha dejado de publicarse desde junio hasta hoy. No nos detendremos en la consideración de un incidente que, en pocos meses, se ha quedado ya atrás en nuestra ruta. Un hecho nuevo nos reclama íntegramente: la reaparición

de "AMAUTA". Nos interesa la meta más que el camino, Y queremos supri-
mir las palabras inútiles. La temporal clausura de "Amauta" pertenece a su
biografía mas propiamente que a su vida. *El trabojo intelectual, cuando no es
metafísico sino dialéctico, vale decir histórico, tiene sus riesgos. ¿Para quien no
es evidente, en el mundo contemporáneo, un nuevo género de accidente del
trabajo?*
La vida de las clásicas "oposiciones" criollas era solo una serie de dramáticas
protestas. *La protesta, primero por abuso, enseguida por desuso, está hoy en el
Perú desacreditada.* Escondía, en el fondo, cierta insolvencia ideológica que
necesitaba, como la insolvencia artística del teatro malo, disimularse con la
bravata, la intriga y el "latiguillo". Donde ántes se ponía declamación, hay que
poner ahora pensamiento. Después de todo, es una ganacia. La palabra que se
contentaba con un servicio anecdótico requiere ahora calidad histórica. Ganare-
mos en ideas-gérmenes, en ideas-valores, lo que perdamos en artículos de fondo
y en frases lapidarias. Si ésto, en nuestro caso, pudiese ser pérdida.
No es ésta una resurrección. "Amauta" no podía morir. *Habría siempre
resucitado al tercer día.* No ha vivido nunca tanto, dentro y fuera del Perú,
como en estos meses de silencio. La hemos sentido defendida por los mejores espíritus de Hispano-América.
Desde las páginas del periódico que Eugenio D' Ors ha llamado "una institu-
cion del Espíritu", he agradecido los magníficos testimonios de solidaridad de
los intelectuales argentinos y uruguayos, del grupo minoritario cubano, de
Garcia Monje y su "Repertorio Americano", etc. Y, en su oportunidad, des-
mentí, en una carta a la prensa de Lima y otra a la prensa latino-americana, las
acusaciones lanzadas contra "Amauta" y sus redactores.
No tengo casi otra cosa que decir en esta nota de reaparición o continuación,
sino que reitero mi reconocimiento a los que, en el Perú y en América, han alen-
tado mi fé y sostenido mi esperanza. Lo demás, lo saben los lectores. Suprima-
mos, repito, las palabras inútiles. [italics added]

[23] Letter to Samuel Glusberg in Buenos Aires. Dated Lima: April 30,
1927. This letter is also reproduced in the following: Mariátegui, *Signos y
obras* (Lima: 1959), on the inside covers. Also in *Babel* (Buenos Aires: 1927).

. . . Con el sector político con el que no me entenderé nunca es el otro: el del
reformismo mediocre, el del socialismo domesticado, el de la democrácia farisea.
*Además, si la revolución exige violencia, autoridad, disciplina, estoy por la
violencia, por la autoridad, por la disciplina. Las acepto, en bloque, con todos
sus horrores, sin reservas cobardes.* [Italics added]

[24] Mariátegui, "Aniversario y balance," *Amauta*, Vol. 3, No. 17 (Lima:
September, 1928), pp. 1–3.

"Amauta" no es una diversión ni un juego de intelectuales puros: profesa una
idea histórica, confiesa una fé áctiva y multitudinaria, obedece a un movimiento
social contemporáneo. En la lucha entre dos sistemas, entre dos ideas, no se nos

ocurre sentirnos expectadores ni inventar un tercer término. La originalidad a ultranza, es una preocupación literaria y anárquica. En nuestra bandera, inscribimos esta sola, sencilla y grande palabra: Socialismo. *(Con este lema afirmamos absoluta independencia frente a la idea de un Partido Nacionalista pequeño burgués y demagógico.* [Italics added]

[25] Ibid, p. 2.

El trabajo de definición ideológica nos parece cumplido. . . . La primera jornada de "Amauta" ha concluido. En la segunda jornada, no necesita ya llamarse revista de la "nueva generación", de la "vanguardia", de las "izquierdas". Para ser fiel a la Revolución, le basta ser una revista socialista.

[26] Mariátegui, "Sobre el problema indígena," *Labor,* No. 1 (Lima: November 10, 1928), p. 6. "Prensa de doctrina y prensa de información," *Labor,* No. 2 (Lima: November 24, 1928), p. 2.

CHAPTER 7—Notes

[1] José Carlos Mariátegui, *Defensa del Marxismo* 2nd ed.: (Lima: 1964), pp. 104–105.

La posición marxista, para el intelectual contemporáneo, no utopista, es la única posición que ofrece una vía de libertad y de avance. . . . El dogma no es un itinerario sino una brújula en el viaje. Para pensar con libertad, la primera condición es abandonar la preocupación de la libertad absoluta.

[2] The events leading to this censure are meticulously documented in: Ricardo Martínez de la Torre, *Apuntes para una interpretación marxista* . . ., Vol. 2, pp. 409–485. Hereafter cited as *Apuntes.*

[3] The existence of such a manuscript is documented in a series of letters in: *Apuntes,* Vol. 2, pp. 404–409.

[4] Ibid.

[5] Mariátegui, *Siete ensayos de interpretación de la realidad peruana,* 8th ed., (Lima: 1959), p. 8. Hearafter cited as *7 ensayos.*

[6] Mariátegui, "Heterodoxía de la tradición," *Mundial,* Vol. 8, No. 389 (Lima: November 25, 1927).

[7] Mariátegui, "La tradición nacional," *Mundial,* Vol. 8, No. 390 (Lima: December 2, 1927).

[8] *7 ensayos,* p. 8.

No faltan quienes me suponen un europeizante, ajeno a los hechos y las cuestiones de mi pais. Que mi obra se encargue de justificarme, contra esta barata e interesada conjectura. He hecho en Europa mi mejor aprendizaje. Y creo que no hay salvación para Indo-América sin la ciencia y el pensamiento europeos u occidentales. . . . Otra vez repito que no soy un crítico imparcial y objetivo. Mis juicios se nutren de mis ideales, de mis sentimientos, de mis pasiones. Tengo una declarada y enérgica ambición: la de concurrir a la creación del socialismo peruano.

[9] The *indigenista* influence in early 20th century Peruvian thought got its initial impetus from Manuel González Prada. The colonial accounts, however, even in Mariátegui's time, were still the best empirical data on the indigenous peoples.

[10] *7 ensayos,* pp. 9–28.

[11] *7 ensayos,* p. 13.

[12] *7 ensayos,* p. 17.

[13] *7 ensayos,* p. 18.

[14] *7 ensayos,* pp. 20–22.

[15] *7 ensayos,* pp. 24–25.

[16] *7 ensayos,* p. 28.

[17] *7 ensayos,* p. 40.

[18] Ibid. For a detailed population study, see: George Kubler, *The Indian Caste of Peru, 1745–1940* (Smithsonian Institution, Institute of Social Anthropology, Washington, Government Printing Office: 1952). The Black Legend is the name given to Dutch and English accounts of the Spanish Conquest. These accounts, written in the mid-16th century were distortions based on the accounts of the Spanish Dominican friar, Bartolomé de las Casas. Las Casas attempted to prove that the Indian was not a savage, and therefore should be protected by the Spanish Crown. The Dutch and English writers sought to prove that the Spanish had no right to claim the New World for themselves, and that the Spanish, not the Indians, were the savages. The Reformation and the competition for trade and empire were the major causes of the origin of the Black Legend. However untrue, it became a justification for all kinds of activity against Spain, from English and Dutch piracy, to a 19th century rationale for independence. It survives to this day in some form or other in the *indigenista* tradition.

[19] *7 ensayos,* p. 32n.

[20] Ibid.

[21] *7 ensayos,* p. 32n–33n.

[22] *7 ensayos,* p. 41. See also note 18 above.

[23] Ibid.

[24] *7 ensayos,* pp. 42–89.

[25] *7 ensayos,* p. 46.

[26] *7 ensayos,* p. 54.

[27] *7 ensayos,* p. 58.

[28] This introductory essay is reproduced in: Mariátegui, *Ensayos escogidos* (Lima: 1956), pp. 13–14.

[29] *7 ensayos,* pp. 62–63.

[30] *7 ensayos,* p. 66.

[31] *7 ensayos,* pp. 66n–69n.

El comunismo moderno es una cosa distinta del comunismo inkaico. Esto es lo primero que necesita aprender y entender, el hombre de estudio que explora el Twantinsuyo. Uno y otro comunismo son un producto de diferentes experiencias humanas. Pertenecen a distintas épocas históricas. Constituyen la elaboración de disimiles civilizaciones. La de los inkas fué una civilización agraria. La de Marx y Sorel es una civilización industrial. En aquella el hombre se sometía a la naturaleza. . . . El hombre del Twantinsuyo no sentía absolutamente ninguna necesidad de libertad individual. . . . Teocrático y despótico fué ciertamente, el régimen inkaico. Pero este es un rasgo común de todos los regímenes de la antigüedad. . . . El ayllu,—la comunidad—, fue la célula del imperio. Los Inkas hicieron la unidad, inventaron el Imperio; pero no crearon la célula. El Estado jurídico organizado por los Inkas reprodujo, sin duda, el Estado natural preexistente. No lo violentaron nada. . . . En la sociedad inkaica no exista el robo porque no exista la propiedad. O, si se quiere, porque existía una organización socialista de la propiedad.

[32] *7 ensayos,* p. 71.

[33] *7 ensayos,* p. 75.

[34] *7 ensayos,* pp. 84–85.

[35] *7 ensayos,* p. 86 and p. 78n. His final propositions appear on pp. 88–89.

[36] *7 ensayos,* p. 105.

[37] Mariátegui, *La novela y la vida* (Lima: 1959), Part 2, p. 122.

[38] *7 ensayos,* p. 109.

[39] *7 ensayos,* pp. 105–116.

[40] *7 ensayos,* p. 124.

[41] *7 ensayos,* p. 139.

[42] *7 ensayos,* pp. 140–67.

[43] *7 ensayos,* p. 155.

[44] *7 ensayos,* p. 167.

[45] *7 ensayos,* p. 167.

[46] *7 ensayos,* pp. 168–69.

[47] *7 ensayos,* p. 291.

[48] *7 ensayos,* p. 292.

CHAPTER 8—Notes

[1] José Carlos Mariátegui, *Defensa del Marxismo.* 2nd ed. (Lima: 1964), p. 17. The first edition appeared in 1935; few copies are extant. All citations are from the 2nd edition. Hereafter cited as *Defensa.*

[2] *Defensa,* pp. 16, 17.

[3] *Defensa,* p. 17.

[4] *Defensa,* p. 19.

[5] *Defensa,* p. 22.

[6] *Defensa,* p. 24.

[7] *Defensa,* p. 31.

[8] *Defensa,* p. 32.

[9] *Defensa,* p. 36.

[10] *Defensa,* p. 37.

[11] *Defensa,* p. 42.

[12] *Defensa,* p. 40.

[13] *Defense,* p. 49.

[14] Ibid.

[15] *Defensa,* p. 51.

[16] Ibid.

[17] This point will be treated in detail in Chapter 9.

[18] *Defensa,* p. 53.

[19] *Defensa,* p. 56.

[20] Ibid.

[21] *Defensa,* p. 57.

[22] *Defensa,* p. 58.

. . . La táctica marxista es, así, dinámica y dialéctica como la doctrina misma de Marx: la voluntad socialista no se agita en el vacío, no prescinde de la situación preexistente. . . . sino que se adhiere sólidamente a la realidad histórica, mas no resignándose pasivamente a ella; antes bien, reaccionando contra ella siempre mas enérgicamente, en el sentido de reforzar económica y espiritualmente al proletariado, de acentuar en él la conciencia de su conflicto con la burguesía, hasta que habiendo llegado al máximo de la exasperación, y la burguesía al extremo de las fuerzas del régimen capitalista, convertido en un obstáculo para las fuerzas productivas, pueda ser útilmente derribado y sustituido, con ventaja para todos, por el régimen socialista. . . . cada palabra, cada acto del marxismo tiene un acento de fe, de voluntad, de convicción heroica y creadora, cuyo impulso seriá absurdo buscar en un mediocre y pasivo sentimiento determinista.

[23] *Defensa,* pp. 59–61.

Todos los que . . . predican y anuncian un socialismo ético, basado en principios humanitarios. . . . El proletariado sucedía a la burguesía en la empresa civilizadora. Y asumía esta misión, consciente de su responsabilidad y capacidad—adquiridas en la acción revolucionaria y en la usina capitalista—cuando la burguesía, cumplido su destino, cesaba de ser una fuerza de progreso y cultura. . . . Los marxistas no creemos que la empresa de crear un nuevo orden social, superior al orden capitalista, incumba un amorfa masa de parias y oprimidos, guiada por evangélicos predicadores del bién. La energía revolucionaria del socialismo no se alimenta de compasión ni de envidia. En la lucha de clases, donde residen todos los elementos de lo sublime y heroico de su ascensión, el proletariado debe elevarse a un "moral de productores", muy distante y distinta de la "moral de esclavos".

[24] *Defensa,* p. 64.

[25] *Defensa, Ibid.* p. 64.

[26] *Defensa,* p. 73.

[27] *Defensa,* pp. 74–78.

[28] *Defensa,* p. 83.

[29] *Defensa,* p. 84.

[30] *Defensa,* p. 84.

[31] *Defensa,* p. 85.

[32] *Defensa,* p. 91.

Un sentimiento mesiánico, romántico, más o menos difundido en la juventud intelectual de post-guerra, que la inclina a una idea excesiva, a veces delirante, de su misión histórica, influye en la tendencia de esta juventud a encontrar al marxismo más o menos retrasado, respecto de las adquisiciones y exigencias de la "nueva sensibilidad". En política, como en literatura, hay muy poca sustancia bajo esta palabra. Pero esto no obsta para que la "nueva sensibilidad" que en el orden social e ideológico prefiere llamarse "nuevo espíritu", se llegue a hacer un verdadero mito, cuya *justa* evaluación, cuyo estricto análisis es tiempo de emprender, sin oportunistas miramientos.

[33] *Defensa,* p. 93.

[34] *Defensa,* p. 95.

[35] *Defensa,* p. 95.

[36] *Defensa,* p. 95.

[37] *Defensa,* p. 98.

[38] *Defensa,* p. 98.

[39] *Defensa,* p. 104.

[40] *Defensa,* p. 105.

[41] *Defensa,* p. 105.

CHAPTER 9—Notes

[1] José Carlos Mariátegui, "Aniversario y balance," *Amauta,* No. 17 (Lima: September, 1928), pp. 1–3. Hereafter cited as "Aniversario."

[2] The exchange of letters between Mariátegui and Haya de la Torre is reproduced in part in the following: *Apuntes,* Vol. 2, pp. 295–369.

[3] *Apuntes,* Vol. 2, pp. 298–99.

[4] *Apuntes,* Vol. 2, pp. 302–304.

[5] Mariátegui, "Lo que el cable no dice," *Mundial,* Vol. 9, No. 484 (Lima: Sept. 27, 1929).

[6] *Apuntes,* Vol. 2, pp. 335–37.

[7] Mariátegui, "Presentación de 'El Amauta de Atusparia,' por Ernesto Reyna," *Mundial,* Vol. 10, No. 508 (Lima: March 15, 1930).

[8] Mariátegui, "El problema de las elites," *Variedades,* Vol. 24, No. 1036 (Lima: January 7, 1928).

[9] "Aniversario."

[10] *Apuntes,* Vol. 2, pp. 409–485. The three approaches to revolution in Peru were also outlined in much the same form by Eudocio Ravines in an interview, on August 8, 1966.

[11] *Apuntes,* Vol. 2, pp. 398–402. (The program of the party is translated and appears in Appendix 1.)

[12] Once in power, Leguía tried to split the armed forces by playing the navy off against the army. In 1924 he went even further by organizing the *Guardia Civil.* Ostensibily an internal police force founded along the lines of the famous Spanish *Guardia,* it was another counterpoise to the army. Significantly, when Leguía was ousted by the army, the *Guardia Civil* was placed under army command, and converted into a riot force. For a history of this unique organization see: Rómulo Merino Arana, *Historia policial del Perú en la República* (Lima: n.d.).

[13] Mariátegui, "Lo que el cable no dice," *Mundial,* Vol. 9, No. 484 (Lima: September 27, 1929), No. 492 (Lima: November 22, 1929), No. 495 (Lima: December 13, 1929), and Vol. 10, No. 504 (Lima: February 15, 1930).

[14] Luis Alberto Sánchez, *Haya de la Torre ó el político* (Santiago de Chile: 1936), p. 155.

[15] Ibid.

[16] This view held by the Communists in 1928 was explained by Eudocio Ravines in an interview (September 14, 1966) and in the following: cf. Chang-Rodríquez, *La literatura política . . .,* p. 165. Victor Alba, *Historia del comunismo en América Latina* (Mexico: 1954), pp. 69–75.

[17] For Mariátegui's comments on political organization, and his changing views on the Soviet Union see: José Carlos Mariátegui, "Lo que el cable no dice," *Mundial,* Vol. 10, No. 500 (Lima: January 18, 1930). " 'La otra Europa', por Luc Durtain," *Variedades* (Lima: Dec. 8, 1928). "¿Exíste una inquietud propia de nuestra época?", *Mundial,* Vol. 10, No. 510 (Lima: March 29, 1930).

[18] Cf. Cenaro Carnero Checa, *La acción escrita.* . . . *Labor* (Lima: January 19, 1946). This *Labor* was a Communist labor organ. S. Simionov and A. Shulgovsky, "El papel de José Carlos Mariátegui en la formación del partido Comunista del Perú." *Hora del hombre,* Vol. 1, No. 1 (Lima: January, 1960), pp. 65–84. "Mariátegui, los comunistas y los socialistas," *Frente,* Vol. 1, No. 3 (Lima: December, 1931), pp. 207–211.

[19] The site of the Congress apparently shifted from Montevideo to Buenos Aires due to the need for secrecy. I have used the Buenos Aires location for clarity, and because most sources refer to it as the Buenos Aires Congress.

[20] The proceedings of the Congress are documented in: *Apuntes,* Vol. 2, pp. 409–485. When possible, I have checked this record with the official organ of the Communist International for Latin America: *La correspondencia sudamericana* (Buenos Aires: 1926–1930). Numbering is irregular.

[21] This is the opinion of Victor Alba. The records of the Congress also bear this out. Cf. *Apuntes,* Vol. 2, pp. 409–485. Victor Alba, *Historia del comunismo en América Latina* (Mexico: 1954), p. 69.

[22] Interview: Eudocio Ravines, September 14, 1966. *Apuntes,* Vol. 2, pp. 497–508.

[23] *Apuntes,* Vol. 2, p. 508.

[24] Ibid.

CHAPTER 10—Notes

[1] "Entierro del señor José Carlos Mariátegui," *El Comercio* (Lima: April 19, 1930), p. 13.

[2] A sample of these eulogies appears in Chang-Rodríguez, *La literatura política* . . . pp. 200–201.

[3] Interview with Martin Adán. (Lima, Peru: August 23, 1966)

[4] An incisive interview with General Velasco Alvarado appears in: "Peru por fin es libre," *Life en español,* Vol. 34, No. 1 (Mexico, D.F.: July 14, 1969) pp. 14–17.

[5] For information on the background and training of the military government's key personnel see: John M. Baines, "Peru," in Marvin Alisky, ed. *Latin American Government Leaders* (Tempe, Arizona: Center for Latin American Studies, Arizona State University Press, 1970), pp. 32–38.

[6] *El Comercio* No. 70964. (Lima: October 9, 1968), pp. 1–2. *El Comercio* No. 70965. (Lima: October 10, 1968), pp. 1, 5. *La Prensa* Vol. 64, No. 27911. Lima: October 10, 1968), pp. 1–3.

[7] *Latin American Digest* Vol. 4, No. 2. (Tempe, Arizona: November, 1969), p. 6.

[8] Ibid., p. 6.

[9] *Latin American Digest,* Vol. 4, No. 5. (Tempe, Arizona: May, 1970), p. 6.

[10] For a discussion of this point see: Murray Edelman; *The Symbolic Uses of Politics* (Urbana, Ill.: University of Illinois Press, 1964). Also, for a general overview of the Peruvian military see: Luigi R. Einaudi, *The Peruvian Military: A Summary Political Analysis* (Santa Monica, California: Rand Corp., 1969).

Bibliography

GENERAL MATERIALS

Apter, David E. *The Politics of Modernization*. Chicago: University of Chicago Press, 1965.

——. *Ideology and Discontent*. New York: The Free Press, 1964.

Arendt, Hannah. *On Revolution*. New York: The Viking Press, 1965.

——. *The Human Condition*. New York: Doubleday & Co., 1959.

Barbusse, Henrí. *The Inferno*. Translated by Edward J. O'Brien. New York: 1918.

——. *We Others*. Translated by Fitzwater Wray. New York: 1918.

——. *Light*. Translated by Fitzwater Wray. New York: 1919.

——. *Clarté*. Paris: 1919.

——. *Le Couteau entre les Dents*. Paris: 1921.

——. *Chains*. Translated by Stephan H. Guest. 2 Vols. London: 1925.

——. *Jesus*. Translated by Solon Librescot. New York: 1927.

——. *I Saw it Myself*. Translated by Brian Rhys. New York: 1928.

Borkenau, Franz. *World Communism*. New York: W. W. Norton & Co. 1939.

Bottomore, T. B. (tr. & ed.) *Karl Marx: Early Writings*. New York: McGraw-Hill Co., 1964.

Brinton, Crane. *The Anatomy of Revolution*. Englewood Cliffs, N.J.: Prentice-Hall & Co., 1938.

Brogan, D. W. *The Price of Revolution*. New York: Grosset & Dunlap, 1951.

Camus, Albert. *The Rebel*. Translated by Anthony Bower. New York: Random House, 1956.

Camus, Albert. *The Myth of Sisyphus and Other Essays*. Translated by Justin O'Brien. New York: Random House, 1955.

Carr, E. H. *Studies in Revolution*. New York: Grosset & Dunlap, 1964.

Cassirer, Ernst. *An Essay on Man*. New Haven: Yale University Press, 1966.

————. *The Myth of the State*. New Haven: Yale University Press, 1966.

Cohn, Norman. *The Pursuit of the Millenium*. Fairlawn, N.J.: Essential Books, Inc., 1957.

DesRoche, Henrí. "Communisme et Religion." *Europe*. February–March, 1954, pp. 116–32.

Eastman, Max. *Marx and Lenin: The Science of Revolution*. London: George Allen & Unwin, 1926.

Edelman, Murray. *The Symbolic Uses of Politics*. Urbana, Ill.: University of Illinois Press, 1964.

Emerson, Rupert. *From Empire to Nation*. Cambridge, Mass.: Harvard University Press, 1960.

Erikson, Erik H. *Childhood and Society*. New York: W. W. Norton & Co., 1950.

————. *Young Man Luther*. New York: W. W. Norton & Co., 1959.

————. *Ghandi's Truth: On the Origins of Militant Nonviolence*. New York: W. W. Norton & Co., 1969.

Feuer, Lewis S. (ed.). *Marx and Engels: Basic Writings on Politics and Philosophy*. New York: Doubleday & Co., 1959.

Frossard, Ludovic O. *De Juares á Leon Blum*. Paris: 1943.

Gay, Peter. *The Dilemma of Democratic Socialism*. New York: MacMillan Co., 1962.

Geertz, Clifford. "Primordial Sentiments and Civil Politics in the New States." In *Old Societies and New States,* ed by Clifford Geertz. New York: The Free Press of Glencoe, 1963.

Hagen, Everrett. *On the Theory of Social Change*. Homewood, Ill.: The Dorsey Press, 1962.

Hobsbawm, Eric. *Primitive Rebels: Studies in Archaic Forms of Social Movement in the 19th and 20th Centuries*. New York: Frederick A. Praeger Inc., 1963.

Hoffer, Eric H. *The True Believer: Thoughts on the Nature of Mass Movements*. New York: Harper & Row Co., 1951.

Johnson, Chalmers. *Revolutionary Change*. Boston: Little, Brown & Co., 1966.

Joll, James. *The Second International: 1889–1914*. London: 1955.

Kaufmann, Walter. *Existentialism from Dostoevsky to Sartre*. Cleveland, Ohio: World Publishing Co., 1956.

Kautsky, John H. *Political Change in Underdeveloped Countries: Nationalism and Communism*. New York: John Wiley & Sons Inc., 1962.

———. *Communism and the Politics of Development*. New York: John Wiley & Sons, Inc., 1968.

Lasswell, Harold D. *Psychopathology and Politics*. New York: Viking Press, 1960.

Lenin, V. I. *What is to be Done?* New York: 1929.

———. *The State and Revolution*. Moscow: Foreign Languages Publishing House, n.d.

———. *Imperialism, The Highest Stage of Capitalism*. Moscow: Foreign Languages Publishing House, n.d.

Lerner, Daniel J. *The Passing of Traditional Society*. New York: Free Press of Glencoe, 1958.

Lichthiem, George. *Marxism: An Historical and Critical Study*. New York: Frederick A. Praeger, 1963.

Meyer, Alfred G. *Marxism: The Unity of Theory and Practice*. Ann Arbor: University of Michigan Press, 1963.

———. *Leninism*. New York: Frederick A. Praeger, 1957.

Minogue, Kenneth R. *Nationalism*. London: B. T. Batsford Ltd., 1967.

Mosse, George L. *The Culture of Western Europe*. New York: Grosset & Dunlap, 1961.

Ortega y Gasset, José. *Meditaciones del Quijote*. Madrid: 1914.

Ortega y Gasset, José. *The Revolt of the Masses*. New York: W. W. Norton & Co., 1957.

Sorel, Georges. *Reflections on Violence*. Translated by J. Roth and T. E. Hulme. New York: Collier Books, 1961.

Shils, Edward. *The Intellectual Between Tradition and Modernity: The Indian Situation*. The Hague: 1961.

Silvert, Kalman H. *The Conflict Society: Reaction and Revolution in Latin America*. Rev. ed. New York: Harper & Row, 1968.

Tuchman, Barbara W. *The Proud Tower*. New York: The MacMillan Co., 1966.

Tucker, Robert. *Philosophy and Myth in Karl Marx*. New York: Cambridge University Press, 1964.

―――. *The Marxian Revolutionary Idea*. New York: W. W. Norton & Co., 1969.

Tuveson, Ernest L. *Millenium and Utopia*. Berkeley: University of California Press, 1949.

Ulam, Adam B. *The Unfinished Revolution*. New York: Vintage Books, 1964.

Unamuno y Jugo, Miguel de. *The Agony of Christianity*. Translated by Ernest Boyd. New York: 1928.

―――. *Del sentimiento trágico de la vida*. Madrid: 1912.

―――. *La vida de Don Quijote y Sancho*. Madrid: 1961.

Wilson, Edmund. *To the Finland Station*. Garden City, New York: Doubleday, Inc., 1953.

Latin America and Peru: General Materials

Adán, Martin. *La casa de cartón*. Lima, Peru: Ediciones Nuevo Mundo, 1961.

Alba, Victor. *Historia del comunismo en América Latina*. Mexico, D.F.: Ediciones Occidentales, 1954.

Alexander, Robert J. *Communism in Latin America*. New Brunswick, N.J.: Rutgers University Press, 1957.

Alisky, Marvin, ed. *Latin American Government Leaders*. Tempe, Arizona: Center for Latin American Studies, Arizona State University, 1970.

Ángeles Cabellero, César A. *El paisaje en Mariátegui, Vallejo y Cieza de León*. Ica, Peru: 1962.

Argos [Victor Raúl Haya de la Torre]. "Bio-bibliografía de José Carlos Mariátegui." *La Tribuna* 7 [Lima]. January 26, 1964.

Baines, John M. "José Mariátegui and the Ideology of Revolution in Peru." *Rocky Mountain Social Science Journal* 7, No. 2 (October 1970).

Basadre, Jorge. *Historia de la república del Perú.* 2 vols. 3rd ed. Lima: 1946.

──────. *Perú: problema y posibilidad.* Lima: 1931.

Baudin, Louis. *L'Empire Socialiste des Inca.* Paris: 1928.

Bazán, Armando. *Biografía de José Carlos Mariátegui.* Lima: 1939.

Beals, Carlton. *Fire on the Andes.* Philadelphia: 1934.

Belaúnde, Victor Andrés. *Meditaciones Peruanas.* Lima: 1961.

──────. *Mi generación en la universidad.* Lima: 1961.

──────. *La realidad nacional.* Paris: 1931.

──────. *Bolivar and the Political Thought of the Spanish American Revolution.* Baltimore: 1938.

Belaúnde Terry, Fernando. *Peru's Own Conquest.* Lima: American Studies Press, 1965.

Bernstein, Harry. "APRA: A Revolutionary Doctrine in Peru, 1919–1951; an Indo-American Program." *Modern and Contemporary Latin America.* Philadelphia: Lippincott, 1952. pp. 675–85.

Bourricaud, Francois. *Power and Society in Contemporary Peru.* New York: Frederick A. Praeger, 1970.

Carey, James C. *Peru and the United States, 1900–1962.* Notre Dame, Ind.: University of Notre Dame Press, 1964.

Carnero Checa, Genaro. *La acción escrita: José Carlos Mariátegui, Periodista.* Lima: 1964.

Carrión, Benjamin. *Mapa de América.* Madrid: 1930.

Chang-Rodríguez, Eugenio. *La literatura política de González Prada, Mariátegui y Haya de la Torre.* Mexico, D.F.: Colección Studium, 1957.

Chaplin, David. "Peru's Postponed Revolution," *World Politics* 20, No. 3 (April 1968), pp. 393–429.

──────. "Peruvian Social Mobility: Revolutionary and Developmental Potential," *Journal of Inter-American Studies* 10, No. 4 (October, 1968), pp. 547–70.

Chirinos Soto, Enrique. *Actores en el drama del Perú y del mundo.* Lima: Ediciones de Divulgación Popular, 1961.

———. "Mariátegui y la tierra," *La Prensa.* Lima: April 16, 1955. p. 8.

Clissold, Stephan. *Latin America: A Cultural Outline.* New York: Harper & Row, 1965.

Concha, Carlos. "The Reign of Terror in Peru," *Current History* 18 (July 1923), pp. 669–72.

Cox, Carlos Manuel. "Reflexiones sobre José Carlos Mariátegui," *Reportorio Americano* 29 [San José, Costa Rica] (July 14, 1923), pp. 17–19.

Crawford, W. Rex. *A Century of Latin American Thought.* 2nd ed. Cambridge, Mass.: Harvard University Press, 1963.

Davis, Harold E. *Makers of Democracy in Latin America.* Washington, D.C.: 1945.

———. *Latin American Social Thought.* Washington, D.C.: 1961.

Democrácia y trabajo. (Numbering irregular) Lima: 1940–1947. This weekly labor organ has some good background material, especially the following issues: March 10, 1941; December, 1943; January 18, 1944; August 5, 1945.

Dennis, Lawrence J. "What Overthrew Leguía," *The New Republic* 64 (Sept. 17, 1930), p. 118.

Dennis, W. J. *Tacna and Arica.* New Haven, Conn.: Yale University Press, 1931.

Eguren, José María. *Poesías completas.* Lima: 1952.

Einaudi, Luigi R. *The Peruvian Military: A Summary Political Analysis.* Santa Monica, California: Rand Corp., 1969.

"Entierro del señor José Carlos Mariátegui." *El Comercio* [Lima], April 19, 1930, p. 13.

Falcón, Jorge. "José Carlos Mariátegui visto a través de su viuda." *Excelsior* 2 [Lima], No. 35, April 16, 1936, p. 8.

Ferrero, Raúl. *El liberalismo peruano.* Lima: 1958.

Frank, Waldo. "Two Peruvians: Dictator and Poet." *The New Republic.* 67, August 12, 1931, pp. 331–34.

———. *América Hispana.* New York: 1931.

———. "A Great American." *The Nation* 130, No. 3389, June 18, 1930, p. 704.

Garcilaso de la Vega, el Inca. *Comentarios reales de los Incas.* 2 vols. Buenos Aires: 1943.

González Prada, Manuel. *Báladas Peruanas.* Santiago de Chile: 1935.

———. *Páginas libres.* 1st ed. Lima: 1894.

———. *Horas de lucha.* Callao, Peru: 1924.

———. *Anarquía.* Santiago de Chile: 1940.

Haya de la Torre, Victor Raúl. "Nuestro frente intelectual." *Amauta* 1 [Lima], No. 4, December 1926. Amauta appeared from 1926 to 1930. It is a most useful source. However, only articles pertinent to this study have been cited.

———. "Romain Rolland y la América Latina," *Amauta* 1 [Lima], No. 2, October 1926.

———. *Pensamiento político.* 5 vols. Lima: 1961.

———. Discurso y programa de 1931. Lima: 1963.

Hora del hombre. Vol. 1, No. 3. Lima: April, 1960.

"Importancia del Primer Congreso Nacional del PCP." *Labor* [Lima], January 19, 1946. This number of the official organ of the Peruvian Communist Party is dedicated to Mariátegui.

Jones, Wills Knapp. *Behind Spanish Footlights.* Austin, Texas: University of Texas Press, 1966.

Kantor, Harry. *The Ideology and Program of the Peruvian Aprista Movement.* Berkeley: University of California Press, 1953.

———. "Aprismo: Peru's Indigenous Political Theory." *The South Atlantic Quarterly* 53, January 1954, pp. 1–9.

Kubler, George. *The Indian Caste System of Peru, 1754–1940.* Washington, D.C.: Smithsonian Institution, Institute of Social Anthropology, U.S. Government Printing Office, 1952.

"La muerte de José Carlos Mariátegui." *Variedades* 26 [Lima], April 17, 1930, pp. 3–4.

Leguía, Augusto B. *Yo tirano, Yo ladrón : Memorias del Presidente Leguía.* Lima, n.d.

"Leguía, Lincoln or Mussolini of Latin America?" *Literary Digest* 106, September 20, 1930, pp. 32, 34.

"Leguía y Mariátegui," *La Prensa* [Lima], March 7, 1955.

Leguía, Jorge Guillermo. *Hombres e ideas del Perú.* Santiago de Chile: 1941.

"Los documentos comprobatorios de la dirección comunista de APRA." *El Comercio* [Lima], March 31, 1932, p. 15.

Mackey, John. *The Other Spanish Christ.* New York: MacMillan Co., 1933.

"Mariátegui contra Mariátegui," *Excelsior* 2 [Lima], No. 36, April 23, 1936, p. 2.

Marret, Sir Robert H. K. *Peru.* New York: Frederick A. Praeger Co., 1969.

Martínez de la Torre, Ricardo. "¿Y ahora?." *Amauta* 5 [Lima], No. 32, August–September 1930.

————. *Apuntes para una interpretación marxista de la historia social del Perú.* 2nd ed. 4 vols. Lima: 1947–1949.

Mazo, Gabriel del. *La reforma universitaria.* 3 vols. Buenos Aires: 1941.

Mead, Jr., Robert G. "Bibliografía crítica de José Carlos Mariátegui." *Revista hispanoamericana* 27 (1961), pp. 138–142.

McNichol, Robert E. "Intellectual Origins of Aprismo." *Hispanic American Historical Review* 23, No. 3, pp. 424–40.

Mejía Baca, Juan. (ed.) *Manual del elector.* Lima: Libreria Juan Mejía Baca, 1961.

————. (ed) *Los Amautas.* Lima: Librería Juan Mejía Baca, 1965.

Merino Arana, Rómulo. *Historia policial del Perú en la República.* Lima: n.d.

Miró Quesada Laos, Carlos. *Autopsía de los partidos políticos.* Lima: 1961.

More, Federico. "José Carlos Mariátegui y la generación infortunada." *Mundial* 10 [Lima], No. 513, April 19, 1930.

Moreno Sánchez, Manuel. *José Carlos Mariátegui.* Mexico, D.F.: 1937.

Miroshevsky, V. "El populismo en el Perú: papel de Mariátegui en la historia del pensamiento social latino-américano." *Dialéctica* Vol. 1 [Havana], No. 1, May–June 1942, pp. 41–59.

North, Lisa. *Civil-Military Relations in Argentina, Chile and Peru.* Berkeley: University of Califronia Press, 1966.

Núñez Anavitarte, Carlos. *Mariátegui y el descentralismo.* Lima: 1958.

Owens, R. J. *Peru.* London: Oxford University Press, 1963.

Pacheco, Maura. *Nuestra revolución en marcha.* Lima: 1962.

Paredes, Luis. "La religión y Mariátegui." *La Prensa* [Lima], April 16, 1955, p. 8.

Payne, James L. *Labor and Politics in Peru.* New Haven: Yale University Press, 1965.

"Perú por fin es libre." *Life en español* [Mexico, D.F.], July 14, 1969, pp. 14–17. This is an interview by a Life correspondent with General Juan Velasco Alvarado, president of Peru.

Phayre, Ignatius. "Leguía, the Maker of Present-Day Peru." *Current History,* April 30, 1930, pp. 103–107.

Pike, Frederick B. *The Modern History of Peru.* New York: Frederick A. Praeger Co., 2nd ed., 1969.

Poemas a Mariátegui. Lima: Empresa Editora Amauta, 1959.

Poppino, Rollie. *International Communism in Latin America: A History of the Movement.* New York: Free Press of Glencoe, 1964.

Prado, Jorge del. "Mariátegui, Marxista Leninista." *Democrácia y trabajo* 88 [Lima], Dec. 1, 1943.

——. *Mariátegui y su obra.* Lima: 1946.

Quijaro, Aníbal. (ed.). *José Carlos Mariátegui: Ensayos escogidos.* Lima: 1956.

Rachitoff, Infantas, Luis. *¿Viéne el comunismo?* Lima: n.d.

Ravines, Eudocio. *The Yenan Way.* New York: 1951.

——. *El momento político.* Lima: 1945.

Reedy, Daniel R. "The Cohesive Influence of José Carlos Mariátegui on Peruvian Art and Politics." *Artists and Writers in the Evolution of Latin America,* edited by Edward D. Terry. University, Alabama: the University of Alabama Press, 1969.

Rouillon, Guillermo. *Bio-bibliografía de José Carlos Mariátegui.* Lima: Universidad Nacional Mayor de San Marcos, 1963.

niquer, Juan [Mariátegui]. "Glosario de las cosas cotidianas." *La Prensa* [Lima], February 29, 1916, p. 5.

_____. "Nirvana." *Lulu* 2 [Lima], No. 5, July 20, 1916, p. 9.

_____. "Afirmación," & "Fantasía lunática." *El Tiempo* [Lima], July 28, 916, p. 8.

riátegui, José Carlos, "Los salmos del dolor." *Colónida* 1 [Lima], N March 16, 1916, pp. 26–27.

niquer, Juan. [M······gui]. "U···

Sánchez, Luis Alberto. "Martiátegui y Valdelomar." *Mundial* 10 [Lima], No. 514, April 26, 1930.

_____. *Don Manuel*. Santiago de Chile: 1937.

_____. *Haya de la Torre ó el político*. Santiago de Chile: 1936.

_____. *Aprismo y religión*. Lima: 1933.

_____. *Haya de la Torre y el APRA*. Santiago de Chile: 1955.

"Señor José Carlos Mariátegui, Director de 'Amauta.'" *Variedades* 25 [Lima], No. 1096, March 6, 1929.

Sigmund, Paul E., ed. *Models of Political Change in Latin America*. New York: Frederick A. Praeger Co., 1970.

Silva Villacorta, Pablo. ¿ *A dónde van las ideas de Haya de la Torre?* Lima: 1966.

Simionov, S. and Shulgovsky, A. "El papel de José Carlos Mariátegui en la formación del Partido Comunista del Perú." *Hora del Hombre* 1 [Lima], No. 1, January 1960.

Solís, Abelardo. *Ante el problema agrario en el Perú*. Lima: 1928.

Stuart, Graham H. *The Tacna-Arica Dispute*. Boston: World Peace Foundation Pamphlets, 1927.

_____. *The Governmental System of Peru*. Washington, D.C.: Carnegie Institution, 1925.

Tamayo Vargas, Agusto. "Herencia de José Carlos Mariátegui." *Hora del Hombre* 1 [Lima], No. 2, February 1960.

Tauro, Alberto. *Amauta y su influencia*. Lima: Empresa Editora Amauta, 1960.

Ugarte, César Antonio. "La política agraria en la república," *Mercurio Peruano*. Vol. 6. No. 59. Lima: May, 1923, pp. 673–76.

Valcárcel, Luis. *Tempestad en los Andes*. 1st ed. Lima: 1927.

_____. *Ruta cultural del Perú*. 3rd ed. Lima: 1965.

Valdelomar, Abraham. *Obras escogidas*. 1st ed. Lima: 1947.

Vargas, J. "En defensa de José Carlos Mariátegui, Marxista." *Claridad* 13 [Buenos Aires], No. 280 (1934).

_____. "José Carlos Mariátegui en la realidad de América Latina." *Claridad* 15 [Buenos Aires], Nos. 304–305 (1936).

Vargas Ugarte, Ruben. *Manual de estudios peruanistas*. 4th ed. Lima: 1959.

Villanueva, Victor. *El militarismo en el Perú*. Lima: 1962.

Watt, Stewart. *The Chinese Bondage in Peru*. Durham, N.C.: Duke University Press, 1951.

Wiesse, María. *José Carlos Mariátegui: Etapas de su vida*. Lima: Ediciones Hora del Hombre, 1945.

Zea, Leopoldo. *The Latin American Mind*. Translated by James H. Abott and Lowell Dunham. Norman, Oklahoma: University of Oklahoma Press, 1963.

Zulen, Dora Mayer de. *El desarrollo de las ideas avanzadas en el Perú*. Callao, Peru: 1934.

Interviews

Martin Adán, Lima, Peru—August 23, 1966.

Ana Mariátegui Chiappe, Lima, Peru—August 8 and Sept. 1, 1966.

Eudocio Ravines, Lima, Peru—Sept. 14, 1966.

Guillermo Rouillon, Lima Peru—August 24, Sept. 2, Sept. 15, and Sept. 30, 1966.

WORKS OF JOSÉ CARLOS MARIÁTEGUI
(Articles listed in chronological order)

Mariátegui, José Carlos. *La escena contemporánea*. 2nd ed. Lima: Empresa Editora Amauta, 1959.

————. *Siete ensayos de interpretación de la realidad peruana*. 8th ed. Lima: Empresa Editora Amauta, 1963.

————. *Seven Interpretive Essays on Peruvian Reality*. Introduction by Jorge Basadre. Translated by Marjory Urquidi. Austin: University of Texas Press, 1971.

————. *El alma matinal*. 2nd ed. Lima: Empresa Editora Amauta, 1959.

————. *La novela y la vida*. 2nd ed. Lima: Empresa Editora Amauta, 1959.

————. *Defensa del Marxismo*. 2nd ed. Lima: Empresa Editora Amauta, 1959.

————. *El artista y la época*. 1st ed. Lima: Empresa Editora Amauta, 19

————. *Signos y obras*. 1st ed. Lima: Empresa Editora Amauta, 1959.

————. *Historia de la crisis mundial*. 1st ed. Lima: Empresa Editora Amauta, 1959.

————. *Temas de nuestra América*. 1st ed. Lima: Empresa Editora Amauta, 1960.

———— *...forma universitaria*. Buenos Aires: 1928.

... santa." *La Prensa* [Lima], A

_____. _La re[...]_

Croniquer, J. [Mariátegui]. "La sema[...] [...] [...]
11, 1914, pp. 1–2.

_____. "El suceso del día." _La Prensa,_ April 28, 1914, p. 3.

_____. "Sobre la prisión del Sr. Vidal." _La Prensa,_ June 20, 1914, p. 1.

_____. "Entre salvajes." _La Prensa,_ July 19, 1914, p. 2.

_____. "Cuenta al cable." _La Prensa,_ August 1, 1914.

_____. "La muerte de Juarès." _La Prensa,_ August 3, 1914, p. 9.

_____. "El rey de Bélgica." _La Prensa,_ October 18, 1914, p. 2.

_____. "La procession tradicional." _La Prensa,_ October 20, 1914, p. 3.

J. C. [Mariátegui]. "El año universitario." _La Prensa:_ January 5, 1915, p. 2.

Croniquer, J. [José Carlos Mariátegui]. "El ocaso de una gloria." _La Prensa,_ February 24, 1915, p. 8.

_____. "Pierre Loti en la guerra." _La Prensa,_ March 20, 1915, p. 2.

_____. "Viendo la cuaresma." _La Prensa,_ March 28, 1915, p. 2.

Croniquer, Juan. [Mariátegui]. "El homenaje a Guisse," _La Prensa,_ April 17, 1915, p. 2.

_____. "D'Annunzio y la guerra." _La Prensa,_ April 27, 1915, p. 1.

_____. "El mal del siglo." _La Prensa,_ April 29, 1915, p. 2.

_____. "La inquisición de Até." _La Prensa,_ May 2, 1915, p. 2.

_____. "Las mujeres pacificistas." _La Prensa,_ May 3, 1915, p. 1.

Camomille, Monsieur de [Mariátegui]. "La reunión del domingo 22." _El Turf_ 2 [Lima], No. 21, August 28, 1915, pp. 3 & 7.

————. [Mariátegui]. "Un incendio a media noche." *El Tiempo* [Lima], August 10, 1916, p. 2.

————. "Elogio de la celda ascética." *El Tiempo* August 28, 1916, p. 3.

[Mariátegui]. "La primavera." *El Tiempo,* September 17, 1916, p. 1.

Croniquer, Juan [Mariátegui]. "La generación literaria de hoy." *El Tiempo* [Lima], October 2, 1916, pp. 2–3.

[Mariátegui]. "Interrogaciones," *El Tiempo,* October 3, 1916, p. 2.

————. "Monotonía." *El Tiempo,* October 9, 1916, p. 1.

Jack [Mariátegui]. "Sensaciones." *El Turf* 3 [Lima], No. 60, October 28, 1916, p. 19.

[Mariátegui]. "El porvenir." *El Tiempo* [Lima], January 22, 1917, p. 1.

————. "Estremecimiento." *El Tiempo,* February 13, 1917, p. 2.

————. "La cara al pasado." *El Tiempo,* March 1, 1917, p. 1.

El Cronista Criollo [Mariátegui]. "La procesión tradicional es un desfile místico y suntuoso." *La Crónica* [Lima], April 10, 1917, pp. 12–13.

[Mariátegui]. "Mayo nacional." *El Tiempo* [Lima], May 1, 1917, p. 2.

————. "La voz de Leguía." *El Tiempo,* May 2, 1917, p. 1.

————. "La ciudad triste." *El Tiempo,* June 11, 1917, p. 1.

————. "Postura inminente." *El Tiempo,* July 3, 1917, p. 1.

Croniquer, Juan [Mariátegui]. "Norka Rouskaya." *El Tiempo,* October 29, 1917, p. 3.

Mariátegui, José Carlos. "El asunto de Norka Rouskaya." *El Tiempo,* November 10, 1917, pp. 2–3.

[Mariátegui]. "Miscelanía criolla." *El Tiempo,* November 18, 1917, p. 1.

———. "Maximilianismo peruano." *El Tiempo,* December 30, 1917, p. 1. Mariátegui replies to the charge made by *El Comercio* that he is a Bolshevik.

———. "Año nuevo." *El Tiempo,* Jan. 1, 1918, p. 1.

———. "Fé liberal." *El Tiempo,* February 3, 1918, pp. 1 & 2.

———. "Leguía viene." *El Tiempo,* March 6, 1918, p. 1.

———. "Lo mismo que ayer." *El Tiempo,* April 1, 1918, p. 1.

———. "Bolshevikis aquí." *El Tiempo,* April 9, 1918, p. 1.

———. "Estamos conspirando." *El Tiempo,* May 27, 1918, p. 1.

———. "A lo lejos . . .," *El Tiempo,* June 5, 1918, p. 1.

———. "La ciudad y las sierras." *El Tiempo,* June 21, 1918, p. 1.

———. "Nuestros carlistas." *El Tiempo,* July 20, 1918, p. 2.

———. "El jóven Perú." *El Tiempo,* September 20, 1918, p. 2.

———. "Partidos militantes." *El Tiempo,* September 26, 1918, p. 1.

———. "Primera jornada." *El Tiempo,* September 30, 1918, p. 1.

———. "Gesto de combate." *El Tiempo,* October 4, 1918, p. 2.

———. "Dias electorales." *El Tiempo,* October 7, 1918, p. 1.

———. "Voto sensacional." *El Tiempo,* October 10, 1918, p. 2.

———. "Paz en la tierra." *El Tiempo,* October 14, 1918, p. 1.

———. "Papeles, papeles, papeles." *El Tiempo,* October 26, 1918, p. 1.

———. "Un día grande." *El Tiempo,* November 12, 1918, p. 2.

———. "Compás de espera." *El Tiempo,* December 30, 1918, p. 1.

Jack [Mariátegui]. "La Entente y los Soviet." *El Tiempo,* July 9, 1920, p. 7.

Croniquer, Juan [Mariátegui]. "Los culpables de la guerra." *El Tiempo,* July 14, 1920, p. 2.

Jack [Mariátegui]. "Las fuerzas socialistas italianas." *El Tiempo,* July 28, 1920, p. 2.

Croniquer, Juan [Mariátegui]. "El divorcio en Italia." *El Tiempo,* October 10, 1920, p. 7. Letter dated Florence, June 30, 1920.

Jack [Mariátegui]. "Benedetto Croce y el Dante." *El Tiempo*, December 9, 1920, p. 5. Letter dated Genoa, August 14, 1920.

Mariátegui, José Carlos. "Cartas de Italia." *El Tiempo*, February 6, 1921, p. 2.

———. "D'Annunzio despues de la epopeya." *El Tiempo*, June 5, 1921.

———. "El cisma socialista." *El Tiempo*, June 12, 1921, p. 7.

Croniquer, Juan [Mariátegui]. "Algo sobre el fascismo." *El Tiempo*, June 29, 1921, p. 3.

Mariátegui, José Carlos. "Aspectos viejos y nuevos del futurismo." *El Tiempo*, August 3, 1921.

———. "El Vaticano y el Quirinal." *El Tiempo*, August 30, 1921.

———. "La casa de los ciegos de la guerra." *El Tiempo*, September 10, 1921, p. 7.

———. "El partido socialista italiano y la III internacional." *El Tiempo*, November 3, 1921, p. 6.

———. "El hambre en Rusia," *El Tiempo*, November 17, 1921, p. 4.

———. "Humo Blanco, habemus Papam." *El Tiempo*, April 7, 1922, p. 5.

———. "El ocaso de la civilización europea." *Claridad* 1 [Lima], No. 1, May 1, 1923, pp. 16–18.

Claridad was a monthly journal published in 1923 and 1924. Directed by Haya de la Torre, it was the organ of the nascent *Frente Único*. Numbering and dates are irregular.

———. "La crisis universitaria." *Claridad* 1, No. 2, n.d., pp. 3–4.

———. "Las voces del tiempo: las Universidades Populares." *Claridad* 1, No. 4, n.d., p. 5.

———. "Palabras de Mariátegui." *Claridad* 2, No. 6, September, 1924?, pp. 1–2.

———. " 'Vanguardia', Semanario de renovación ideológica." *El Comercio*, [Lima], November 7, 1923, p. 2.

———. "Giovani Papini." *Variedades* 19 [Lima], No. 820, November 17, 1923, p. 3262.

———. "La transformación del mundo oriental." *Variedades* 19, No. 825, December 22, 1923, p. 3611.

———. "México y la revolución." *Variedades* 20, No. 827. January 5, 1924, p. 96.

———. "La revolución y la reacción en Bulgaria." *Variedades* 20, No. 828, January 12, 1924, p. 96.

———. "El asunto de 'Claridad'." *La Crónica* 12, No. 4253, January 15, 1924, p. 2.

———. "Tchitcherin y la política exterior de los Soviets." *Variedades* 20, No. 834, February 23, 1924, p. 461.

———. "El fascismo y el monarquismo en Alemania." *Variedades* 20, No. 839, March 29, 1924, p. 782.

———. "Clarté." *Variedades* 20, No. 840, April 5, 1924, pp. 841–43.

———. "Trotsky." *Variedades* 20, No. 842. April 19, 1924, pp. 981–84.

———. "¡Trabaiadores manuales e intelectuales!" *El Obrero Textile* 5 [Lima], No. 59, May 1, 1924, p. 3.

———. "El 1º de mayo y el Frente Único Proletario." *El Obrero Textile* 5, No. 59, May 1, 1924, p. 2.

———. "La crisis de la democracia." *Mundial* 5 [Lima], No. 235, September 14, 1924.

———. "Proyecciones del proceso Matteoti." *Mundial* 5, No. 238, September 26, 1924.

———. "La urbe y el campo." *Mundial* 5, No. 229, October 3, 1924. The numbering of *Mundial* is irregular.

———. "La revolución china," *Variedades* 20, No. 866, October 4, 1924, p. 2468.

———. "Nacionalismo e Internacionalismo," *Mundial* 5, No. 230, October 14, 1924.

———. "Pasadismo y futurismo." *Mundial* 5, No. 233, October 31, 1924.

———. "La libertad en el Egipto." *Variedades* 20, No. 870, November 1, 1924, p. 2730.

———. "El problema primario del Perú." *Mundial* [Número extraordinario], December 9, 1924.

———. "El partido bolchevique de Trotzky." *Variedades* 21, No. 883, January 31, 1925, p. 225.

———. "Sun Yat Sen." *Variedades* 21, No. 891, March 28, 1925, p. 655.

———. "¿Existe un pensamiento Hispano-Americano?" *Mundial* 6, No. 255, May 1, 1925.

———. "Ibero-Americanismo y Pan-Americanismo." *Mundial* 6, No. 255, May 8, 1925.

———. "La política francesa." *Variedades* 21, No. 897, May 9, 1925, p. 928.

———. "La enseñanza y la economía." *Mundial* 6, No. 259, May 29, 1925.

———. "Instantáneas." *Variedades* 21, No. 901, June 6, 1925.

———. "Hacia el estudio de los problemas peruanos." *Mundial* 6, No. 265, July 10, 1925.

———. "El imperialismo y la China." *Variedades* 21, No. 906, July 11, 1925. p. 1570.

———. "Nacionalismo realista." *Mundial* 6, No. 266, July 17, 1925.

———. "El hecho económico en la historia peruana." *Mundial* 6, No. 270, August 14, 1925.

———. "El rostro y el alma del Twantinsuyo." *Mundial* 6, No. 274, September 11, 1925.

———. "Pesimismo de la realidad y optimismo del ideal." *Mundial* 6, No. 271, August 21, 1925.

———. "La máscara y el rostro." *Mundial* 6, No. 275, September 18, 1925.

———. "El Indio de la República." *Mundial* 6, No. 276. Lima: September 25, 1925.

———. "El progreso nacional y el capital humano." *Mundial* 6, No. 278, October 9, 1925.

———. "La tragedia del sábado." *Mundial* 6, No. 282, November 6, 1925.

———. "Nacionalismo y vanguardismo." *Mundial* 6, No. 285, November 27, 1925.

———. "Nacionalismo y vanguardismo en la literatura y ςn el arte." *Mundial* 6, No. 286, December 4, 1925.

———. "El nuevo espíritu y la escuela." *Mundial* 6, No. 287, December 11, 1925.

_____. "El problema de la estatística." *Mundial* 6, No. 290, January 1, 1926.

_____. "Economía colonial." *Mundial* 6, No. 291. Lima: January 8, 1926.

_____. "¿Cómo escribe usted?" *Variedades* 22, No. 932, January 9, 1926, pp. 11–12.

_____. "La conscripción vial." *Mundial* 6, No. 299, Lima: March 5, 1926.

_____. "El proceso de la literatura peruana." *Mundial* 7, No. 302, March 26, 1926.
This is the second of six articles which appeared under the same title in Numbers 300 through 305 of *Mundial*.

_____. "La nueva Rusia y los emigrados." *Variedades* 22, No. 946, April 17, 1926.

_____. "Las nuevas jornadas de la revolución China." *Variedades* 22, No. 947, April 24, 1926.

_____. "El proceso de la literatura peruana." *Mundial* 7, No. 314, June 18, 1926.

_____. "La agitación revolucionaria en España." *Variedades* 12, No. 958, July 10, 1926.

_____. "Una encuesta á José Carlos Mariátegui." *Mundial* 7, No. 319, July 23, 1926.

_____. "La reacción en México." *Variedades* 22, No. 962, August 7, 1926.

_____. "Después de la muerte de Dzerjinsky." *Variedades* 22, No. 964, August 21, 1926.

_____. "Presentación." *Amauta* 1, [Lima], No. 1, September, 1926, p. 3.

_____. "L' agonie du Christianisme." *Amauta* 1, No. 1, September, 1926, pp. 3–4.

_____. "La poesía de Magda Portal." *Mundial* 7, No. 325, September 3, 1926.

_____. "La evolución de la economía peruana." *Amauta* 1, No. 2, October, 1926, pp. 29–32.

_____. "Arte, revolución y decadencia." *Amauta* 1, No. 3, November, 1926, pp. 26–29.

————. "Regionalismo y centralismo." *Amauta* 1, No. 4, December, 1926, pp. 25–30.

————. "La historia económica social." *Mundial* 7, No. 339, December 10, 1926.

————. "Aspectos del problema indígena." *Mundial* 7, No. 340, December 17, 1926.

————. "La institución de la República." *Mundial* 7, No. 341, December 24, 1926.

————. "Política uruguaya." *Variedades* 23, No. 983, January 1, 1927.

————. "El Cuzco y el Indio." *Mundial* 7, No. 343, January 7, 1927.

————. "El movimiento socialista en el Japón." *Variedades* 23, No. 984, January 8, 1927.

————. "El imperialismo yanqui en Nicaragua." *Variedades* 23, No. 986, January 22, 1927.

————. "Mensaje al Congreso Obrero." *Amauta* 2, No. 5, January, 1927, pp. 35–36.

————. "Nota polémica." *Amauta* 2, No. 6, February, 1927, p. 29.

————. "El problema de la China." *Variedades* 23, No. 989, February 12, 1927.

————. "El Congreso anti-imperialista de Bruselas." *Variedades* 23, No. 890, February 19, 1927.

————. "Polémica finita." *Amauta* 2, No. 7, March, 1927, pp. 37–39.

————. "Indigenismo y socialismo: Intermezzo polémico." *Amauta* 2, No. 7, March, 1927, pp. 37–39.

————. "La toma de Shanghai." *Variedades* 22, No. 996, April 2, 1927.

————. "La decadencia de Inglaterra." *Variedades* 23, No. 1003, May 21, 1927.

————. "Sobre el fraguado complot comunista." *La Crónica* 14, No. 7072, June 12, 1927, p. 15.

————. "La organización de los empleados." *Mundial* 8, No. 384, October 21, 1927.

————. "'Indología' por José Vasconcelos." *Variedades* 23, No. 1025, October 22, 1927.

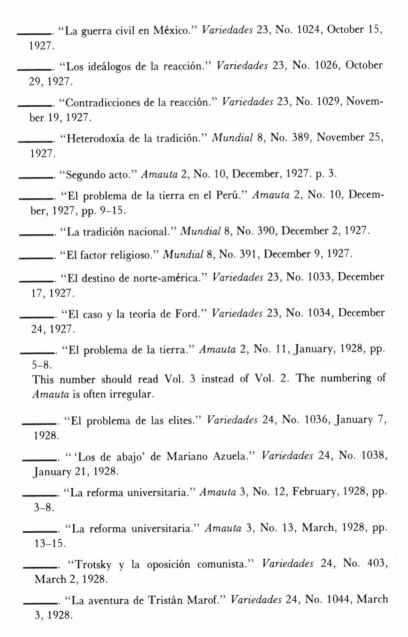

———. "La guerra civil en México." *Variedades* 23, No. 1024, October 15, 1927.

———. "Los ideálogos de la reacción." *Variedades* 23, No. 1026, October 29, 1927.

———. "Contradicciones de la reacción." *Variedades* 23, No. 1029, November 19, 1927.

———. "Heterodoxía de la tradición." *Mundial* 8, No. 389, November 25, 1927.

———. "Segundo acto." *Amauta* 2, No. 10, December, 1927. p. 3.

———. "El problema de la tierra en el Perú." *Amauta* 2, No. 10, December, 1927, pp. 9–15.

———. "La tradición nacional." *Mundial* 8, No. 390, December 2, 1927.

———. "El factor religioso." *Mundial* 8, No. 391, December 9, 1927.

———. "El destino de norte-américa." *Variedades* 23, No. 1033, December 17, 1927.

———. "El caso y la teoría de Ford." *Variedades* 23, No. 1034, December 24, 1927.

———. "El problema de la tierra." *Amauta* 2, No. 11, January, 1928, pp. 5–8.
This number should read Vol. 3 instead of Vol. 2. The numbering of *Amauta* is often irregular.

———. "El problema de las elites." *Variedades* 24, No. 1036, January 7, 1928.

———. " 'Los de abajo' de Mariano Azuela." *Variedades* 24, No. 1038, January 21, 1928.

———. "La reforma universitaria." *Amauta* 3, No. 12, February, 1928, pp. 3–8.

———. "La reforma universitaria." *Amauta* 3, No. 13, March, 1928, pp. 13–15.

———. "Trotsky y la oposición comunista." *Variedades* 24, No. 403, March 2, 1928.

———. "La aventura de Tristán Marof." *Variedades* 24, No. 1044, March 3, 1928.

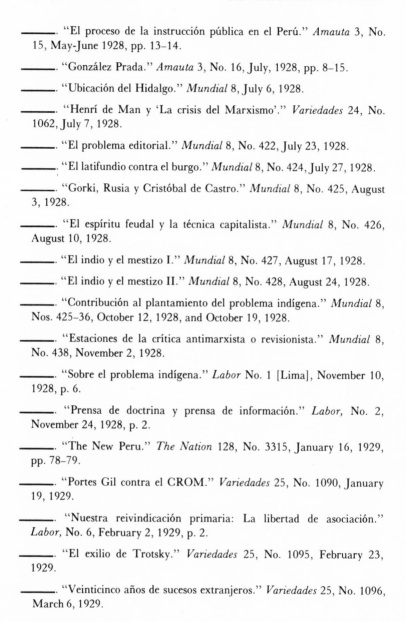

————. "El proceso de la instrucción pública en el Perú." *Amauta* 3, No. 15, May-June 1928, pp. 13–14.

————. "González Prada." *Amauta* 3, No. 16, July, 1928, pp. 8–15.

————. "Ubicación del Hidalgo." *Mundial* 8, July 6, 1928.

————. "Henrí de Man y 'La crisis del Marxismo'." *Variedades* 24, No. 1062, July 7, 1928.

————. "El problema editorial." *Mundial* 8, No. 422, July 23, 1928.

————. "El latifundio contra el burgo." *Mundial* 8, No. 424, July 27, 1928.

————. "Gorki, Rusia y Cristóbal de Castro." *Mundial* 8, No. 425, August 3, 1928.

————. "El espíritu feudal y la técnica capitalista." *Mundial* 8, No. 426, August 10, 1928.

————. "El indio y el mestizo I." *Mundial* 8, No. 427, August 17, 1928.

————. "El indio y el mestizo II." *Mundial* 8, No. 428, August 24, 1928.

————. "Contribución al plantamiento del problema indígena." *Mundial* 8, Nos. 425–36, October 12, 1928, and October 19, 1928.

————. "Estaciones de la crítica antimarxista o revisionista." *Mundial* 8, No. 438, November 2, 1928.

————. "Sobre el problema indígena." *Labor* No. 1 [Lima], November 10, 1928, p. 6.

————. "Prensa de doctrina y prensa de información." *Labor,* No. 2, November 24, 1928, p. 2.

————. "The New Peru." *The Nation* 128, No. 3315, January 16, 1929, pp. 78–79.

————. "Portes Gil contra el CROM." *Variedades* 25, No. 1090, January 19, 1929.

————. "Nuestra reivindicación primaria: La libertad de asociación." *Labor,* No. 6, February 2, 1929, p. 2.

————. "El exilio de Trotsky." *Variedades* 25, No. 1095, February 23, 1929.

————. "Veinticinco años de sucesos extranjeros." *Variedades* 25, No. 1096, March 6, 1929.

_____. "Orígenes y perspectivas de la insurrección mexicana." *Variedades* 25, No. 1099, March 27, 1929.

_____. "Admonición del 1º de Mayo." *Labor* 8, May 1, 1929, p. 2.

_____. "Andre Chamson y el mito de la nueva generación: La revolución del '19'." *Variedades* 25, No. 1099, March 27, 1929.

_____. "La libertad y el dogma." *Mundial* 9, No. 467, May 31, 1929.

_____. "Rusia y China." *Variedades* 25, No. 1166, July 26, 1929.

_____. "Bourdelle y el anti-Rodin." *Amauta* 4, No. 26, September-October, 1929, pp. 92–94.

_____. "Notas." *Amauta* 4, No. 26, September-October, 1929, pp. 92–94.

_____. "El proletariado contra la guerra." *Labor,* No. 7, August 1, 1929. "Boletin."

_____. "Labor continua." *Labor,* No. 9, August 18, 1929, p. 1.

_____. "Lo que el cable no dice: las elecciones en México." *Mundial* 9, No. 484, September 27, 1929.

_____. "Lo que el cable no dice." *Mundial* 9, No. 490, November 8, 1929. This is part of a series of articles on the "world crisis." Others appeared in the following numbers of *Mundial:* No. 492. November 22, 1929., No. 494. December 6, 1929., No. 495. December 13, 1929., No. 498. January 3, 1930., No. 500. January 18, 1930., No. 504. February 15, 1930., and No. 506. March 1, 1930.

_____. "Presentación de, 'El Amauta Atusparia', por Ernesto Reyna," *Mundial* 10, No. 508, March 15, 1930.

_____. "¿Exíste una inquietud própia de nuestra época?" *Mundial* 10, No. 510, March 29, 1930.

_____. "La crisis mundial y el proletariado peruano." *Amauta* 5, No. 30, April-May, 1930. pp. 5–10.

_____. "La emoción de nuestro tempo," *Amauta* 5, No. 31, June-July, 1930.

Index

founder of APRA, 4, 52; ideology 47, 128; relationship with Communists, 135; relationship with Mariátegui, 27, 47–48, 53, 63, 69–76 79, 81–82, 112, 124, 125–127, 130- 132, 133, 140. *See Also* APRA Mariátegui, José Carlos

Indians; Mariátegui's view of, 56–60, 64, 66, 89, 102; military view of. 146; under Ramón Castilla, 9; population, 12, 89–90; views of González Prada, 13–16. *See also Ayllu;* Castilla, Ramón; Congreso Socialista de Latinoamerica; González Prada; Mariátegui, José Carlos
Ingenieros, José, 57
"International of Thought," 34
Iparraguirre, 73

Jesuits, 85
John of the Cross, Saint, 20
Juarès, Jean, 30, 31
Justo, Juan B., 2

Kautsky, Karl, 42
Kuomintang, 82, 126, 133

Labor (Mariátegui), 77
la Chira, Mariá Amalia (mother of José Carlos Mariátegui), 17, 20, 21, 51, 160 n. 2.
La Convención, 144
LaFarque, Paul, 30
Las Casas, Bartolomé de, 84, 91, 172 n. 8.
Latifundia, 95, 97–98
Leguía, Augusto B.; attack on *Frente Único*, 50–51; closing of *Amauta*, 67–68, 73–74; closing of *Claridad*, 50; closing of *Labor*, 77; coup of 1919, 11, 25; *Leguísmo*, 127; *once-nio*, 13, 131; opposition of Mariátegui, 24, 43, 47, 51, 112, 130, 139; opposition of students and workers

26–28, 46, 51; support of Futurists, 24–25
Lenin, V. I., 72, 91, 104, 129, 140; death, 123; program of, 105, 111, 116, 120; as viewed by Mariátegui, 107–109, 117, 121, 122, 130
Lerner, Daniel J., 5
Liebknicht, Wilhelm, 42
Life of Don Quijote and Sancho, The (Unamuno), 37
Local Workers' Federation, 49
Luxemburg, Rosa, 110

Mao Tse-tung, 104
Mariátegui, Francisco Javier (father of José Carlos Mariátegui), 17, 160 n. 2.
Mariátegui, Guillermina (sister of José Carlos Mariátegui), 20
Mariátegui, José Carlos; death, 139; early years 17–28; indigenous concepts, 44, 57–60, 64, 66, 68, 70, 71, 80, 82–85, 89–92, 93, 96–97, 99–102, 103, 105, 106, 107, 127, 128, 143, 166 n. 25.; influence of González Prada, 27, 56, 69, 124, 130; illness, 51–52, 76, 137; marriage 41; as Marxist theorist, 22, 28, 30–38, 41, 43, 44, 59–60, 80–84, 88, 91, 99–101, 104–123, 131, 140–141, 143; as nationalist, 3, 40–41, 57–61, 71, 90, 105–106, 116, 128, 129, 140–141, 143; pseudonyms, 160 n. 5.; relationship with Haya de la Torre, 27, 47–48, 53, 63, 69–76, 79, 81–82, 112, 124, 125–127, 130–132, 133, 140; religious crisis, 20–21, 28, 38, 95; as revolutionary theorist, 2–7, 34, 38, 41–45, 46–47, 52, 53, 55–61, 64, 67, 69, 72, 76, 77, 79, 82, 83, 86, 90, 91, 93–94, 102, 104, 107–108, 112, 115, 117, 121, 124, 127, 141–143. *See also* D'Annunzio, G.; González Prada; Barbusse; Unamuno; Croce; Valdelomar, A.;